W9-AGT-107

Waley-el-dine Sameh DAILY LIFE IN ANCIENT EGYPT

Waley-el-dine Sameh

DAILY LIFE IN ANCIENT EGYPT

Translated from the German by Michael Bullock

McGRAW-HILL BOOK COMPANY · NEW YORK LONDON TORONTO

My sincere thanks are due to all those whose profound kindness afforded me access to the treasures of antiquity and thus facilitated and encouraged my work. In particular, I should like to thank Dr Anwar Shukri, General Director of the Department of Antiquities and Director of the Egyptian Museum in Cairo, and all the conservators and inspectors of Egyptian antiquities in the country. I owe special thanks to Dr Zaki Y. Saad for valuable information relating to Sakkara. I am also deeply indebted to Professor Abdel Moneim Abu Bakr for his kindness in imparting to me certain facts relating to Upper Egypt, to Professor Joachim Spiegel for his brilliant elucidations of various problems and to Mr Abdel Moneim es Sawi, Under-Secretary of State in the Ministry of Culture for his lively interest in this book.

Library of Congress Catalog Card No. 64-22729
54505
Printed in West Germany

Contents

Introduction	7
Outline map	11
Nature and man	13
The seasons (Agriculture)	31
Handicrafts (Building)	41
Food and drink	59
Dress and the toilet	77
Jewellery and gold	95
The family	105
Music and dancing	123
Writing and scribes	133
Painting	143
Painting with a spatial effect	147
The otherworldly look	151
Chronological table	157
Bibliography	159

To my wife

Introduction

Even in antiquity the monuments of Ancient Egypt aroused the unreserved admiration of Herodotus and other classical authors and right up to the present they have continued to be regarded as the creations of supermen, if not of giants.

The purpose and meaning of these huge constructions, covered with inscriptions, were bound to remain a mystery so long as the inscriptions were undeciphered. The spectator gazes in awe at the objects themselves and is astounded by the mastery of technical problems involved in erecting them. What secret methods enabled the craftsmen of the Nile Valley to work the great blocks of stone and the enormous statues of granite and diorite with tools of comparatively soft bronze? Hewn blocks weighing hundreds of tons were transported for miles from the mountains over desert sand, soft ploughed land and on the Nile. What equipment did they have for this purpose?

Champollion was the first, in 1822, to create a basis for the decipherment of the hieroglyphs by means of the trilingual (hieroglyphs, demotic and Greek) inscription on the Rosetta Stone. Archaeologists began the systematic exploration of a world which for so long had been the object merely of curiosity and amazement. A new science was born: Egyptology.

The connections of the Greeks and the Roman Empire with Egypt belonged to the classical past, Cleopatra's name was linked with vague, romantic notions. Visible witnesses to a vanished empire, the strange obelisks, often bearing decorative carving, tower into the sky of Rome and Constantinople. The modern world found itself confronted by a State that could boast over three thousand years of political and cultural continuity, to say nothing of its prehistoric existence. Admiration for this hitherto unknown people knew no bounds. It became possible to read the documents of a religion whose existence no one had suspected, while highly detailed accounts furnished information about battles, conquests and temporary foreign dominations. The deeds of the pharaohs and their statesmen were numberless, and the heroic lustre of the dynasties that held power caused the nameless millions to be overlooked. Yet it was they who, carrying out the will of their rulers, administrators and priests, produced those astonishing monuments, those works of art in stone, gold, gems, glass and wood.

The subject of this book is the simple man between the desert and the Nile, the creator of all those almost incredible great and small wonders that still delight and astound us—the artist to whom both the technical and the creative aspects of his art were a matter of course, but at the same time a mystic religious duty. For Egyptian man lived a life of double fulfilment: he was the medium through which the testimonies to the immortality of the nation came into being; rarely named, he generally sank into oblivion amidst the infinitely vast mass of his people, a tiny part contributing to a great culture in bronze, stone, word, writing, painting and music.

In addition to this, he found fulfilment in a second way: through his belief in life after death. The religion of the ancient Egyptians was the first in human history to contain the concepts soul, judgment of the soul and the continuation of life in the hereafter. But the right to Paradise had to be won on earth. The path to the judge of souls was long and difficult. The soul had to present him with evidence regarding its earthly acts. It might be declared worthy or cast into everlasting darkness.

With its daily revolution the sun, the seat of the supreme deity, was the symbol of the eternal cycle of dying and self-renewal, of life, death and resurrection. After going down in the west, dying, it wandered as a red disc on the point of extinction, all the time fighting for its life, through the depths of the earth beneath the desert and the Nile, only to rise from the sea in the east to radiant new life next morning. For this journey it made use of the sun-boats, one until morning, the other until

evening. Like the sun, the dead also embarked upon the journey into the Underworld, in order, after passing various tests in the other world, happily to begin a new life.
While still in possession of his full powers, that is to say between the ages of twenty-five and thirty-five, the Egyptian began to see to his "house of eternity." Since time immemorial, tombs were situated at a great distance from dwellings, in the sand of the desert or in the rocky valleys. Thanks to the dry climate of this land of low rainfall, a great many of them remained intact. Apart from the mummy in its sarcophagus, a statue of the dead person in wood or stone stood in the tomb chamber. With a very few exceptions, the individual is portrayed at a timeless age. On the inner walls of the tomb we find ritual representations such as the sealing of the sarcophagus, the funeral procession and, as the culmination, the judgment of the soul. The individual phases undergo certain modifications in the course of time; the dictates of ritual compelled a repetitiveness of rendering that may appear stereotyped to the modern observer. For us the significance of prayer, of moral self-justification before the supreme judge, has paled; but the joyous colours and the astonishing liveliness of the detail continue to exercize their charm throughout the ages.

The Egyptian loved his home above everything, and life seemed to him worth living. By comparison with the neighbouring peoples of that time, his way of life and civilization was of such a high level that, quite rightly, he only felt happy in his own country. Hence it is understandable that an after-life should have been conceived as an idealized counterpart of life on earth. As portrayed in pictures, Paradise, with its trees, animals and water, resembles the earthly environment. Even clothing remains unchanged. In the Next World, the countryman ploughs, sows and reaps without any effort. In Yaru (Paradise) corn grows to three times its earthly height, the ears are big with grain, fruit always ripe for plucking. All earthly cares have vanished. The nobleman rests with his wife in an armchair under the sycamore, breathing the scent of the lotus flower.
Let us return to the justification of the soul. The negative confession of sins was a forerunner of the Ten Commandments: "I have not sinned, have not killed, have not baked sacrificial loaves that were too small, have not taken milk from the child, have not diverted water from my neighbour's field..." and many other things. They were immutable formulae established by religious convention.
Over and above compliance with the priestly behest, the living man had an understandable urge to inform the Judge of Souls and his Assessors of his very personal conduct on earth. Passing beyond the abstract norm of the ritual formula, he proceeded to a concrete, poignantly authentic human statement. The account given by the occupant of the tomb is free from all self-embellishment and often filled with a certain naive pride. Dignitaries liked to have the offering and gifts bestowed upon them by tributaries on behalf of the State carefully depicted. We find frequent portrayals of happy family life and domestic work. Children accompany their father on a hunt or assiduously help with the harvest.
Here the painter and stone-carver no longer drew his inspiration from the mysteries, legends and heroic deeds of the lords of earth and heaven, but from the everyday life of the individual in the crowd. We can see from these pictorial records what made up the Egyptian's true life and destiny. Our eyes, accustomed to the present with its surfeit of technology, see what many thousands of years ago moved man by the Nile, what life and culture, pride and happiness meant to him in his most immediate environment.
These pictures of everyday existence suggested the idea of a collection that would faithfully depict the daily life of the age, further illuminated by means of contemporary tools, utilitarian objects and documents. Additional insight is afforded by the tombs. The road to the Next World was full of

obstacles. Hence the stick and sandals of the deceased were laid beside his sarcophagus. The scribe was given his writing materials, the hunter or warrior their appropriate weapons; women their spindles, jewellery or perfume bottles, in short everything that had been of importance to them during their life on earth. Filled beakers and bowls were set down to provide food and drink for the journey, and finally the tomb chamber was carefully walled up. The open anteroom built on afterwards was provided as a place where the relatives could place offerings of food and other gifts in memory of the dead. The simple earthenware vessels and other utilitarian articles in the tomb-chamber have largely been preserved and provide important information regarding the daily life of the time.

Houses and household effects have not come down to us for the simple reason that, like their occupants, they were not intended to endure. They were made of perishable material, unbaked clay bricks, wood and rushes. Stone, since the Third Dynasty elevated to a symbol of eternity, was reserved for religious buildings, such as tombs, chapels, temples and obelisks, in short for everything connected with the concept of religion.

The purpose of the stone tomb, also called the "house of eternity," was to shelter the mummy for all time. The sumptuous funerary furniture of the nobles is in strange contrast to their modest household effects and utensils. This might easily lead to the mistaken conclusion that, in the hope of a better life in the Next World, the Egyptians lived ascetically. Nothing could be more misleading. They had an entirely positive attitude to life on earth and enjoyed it to the full. Every house had its own garden with a pond, trees and flowers. Behind the house was the courtyard with stables and storehouses. A few houses in Tel el-Amarna were up to three storeys high, as may be seen from reliefs there. As was to be expected, dwellings were situated close to water and the fields, and were therefore acutely exposed to the action of dampness.

The Nile was and is the life-blood of the country. Rainfall is limited to a few days a year. The Nile's tributaries originate from the vast accumulations of water in Central Africa. With the masses of water comes the fertile mud that forms the cultivable soil of Egypt. Following the rainy seasons in the regions of Ethiopia, Lake Victoria and the mountain massif of Ruwenzori, the Nile, depending upon the amount of rainfall, could sink so low that in dry years villages had to be built right on its banks, or might rise so high that whole tracts of land were submerged. At such times, in Upper Eypt, dwellings were erected at the foot of the limestone hills. The unbaked brick offered little resistance to the raging floods, and so whole settlements disappeared, usually to be rebuilt on the same site with the debris of the original village combined with new material. The ceaseless coming and going of men and floods continued right down to our own day, when dams were built.

Objects have been reconstructed by painstakingly fitting together fragments found in ruins, agricultural land and sand. More rarely, well-preserved stonemasons' implements and tools have come to light in quarries.

Tel el-Amarna, the city founded by Akhenaton, far from the old centres, constitutes a fortunate exception. For a brief period, this pharaoh imposed revolutionary changes in the national religion. The priesthood of Karnak, deprived of their prestige, accused him of heresy. After his death, the old priesthood gained power again and caused the destruction of Amarna and its temples. The inhabitants fled from the city. Fortunately for posterity, its destruction was incomplete; no fresh settlements were established on the same site. When Tel el-Amarna was excavated much important information regarding town-planning, drainage systems and domestic architecture came to light.

During the long life of ancient Egypt foreign conquerors, religious struggles and not least time itself contributed to the destruction of religious centres.

The most remarkable factor in the Egyptian world is the spirit of all-embracing order. This order dominates not only the whole organization of the State, but also plays a controlling role in family life. The subjection to discipline, which, in spite of frantic revolutions, religious conflicts and occasional foreign domination, repeatedly re-established itself, is not to be explained solely as a deep-seated ethical outlook. The topography of the country imposed this order as a fundamental necessity without which Egypt could not have survived.

This book aims to provide a realistic picture of the daily life of ancient Egypt based exclusively on contemporary documents and without recourse to any reconstructions, present-day models or conjecture. Similarly no attempt has been made to arrange the reproductions in a chronological sequence. It would have been possible to confine ourselves to a particular period or a particular type of representation. But this would have deprived the reader of outstandingly beautiful, typical depictions and objects from other epochs. The subject under discussion is in any case so excessively rich that limitations were imposed automatically by the nature and dimensions of the book. Important themes have had to be omitted, although daily life was permeated by them: gods and beliefs, astronomy and astrology, birth and death, physicians and medicine—which was very closely linked with the art of embalming —military power, navigation and many other things. In looking at the illustrations we must constantly call to mind that, in so far as we are dealing with the true tomb-chambers with their pictures and *Ka* statues, or with the tombs of the kings, they come from rooms that were walled-up, covered over, deliberately hidden from view for all time. The chambers above ground, on the other hand, stood open to visitors. The contents of the tombs do not represent art in our sense of the word—something intended to be looked at. They are meant for the Next World. And for that reason they are truth itself, plain, unvarnished, poignant in its simplicity. For what would it have profited a man to present untruths to the Judge of the Dead? Faced with death and its inflexible might, the ancient Egyptian acknowledges his human frailty, but also his calm and composure in the shadow of death and life after death, which he recognized as immutable and whose immovable law he bore within and upon him. This knowledge did not bring with it any paralyzing burden of fatalism. Because he looked at it from the viewpoint of death, the ancient Egyptian's avowal of life was unconsciously heroic.

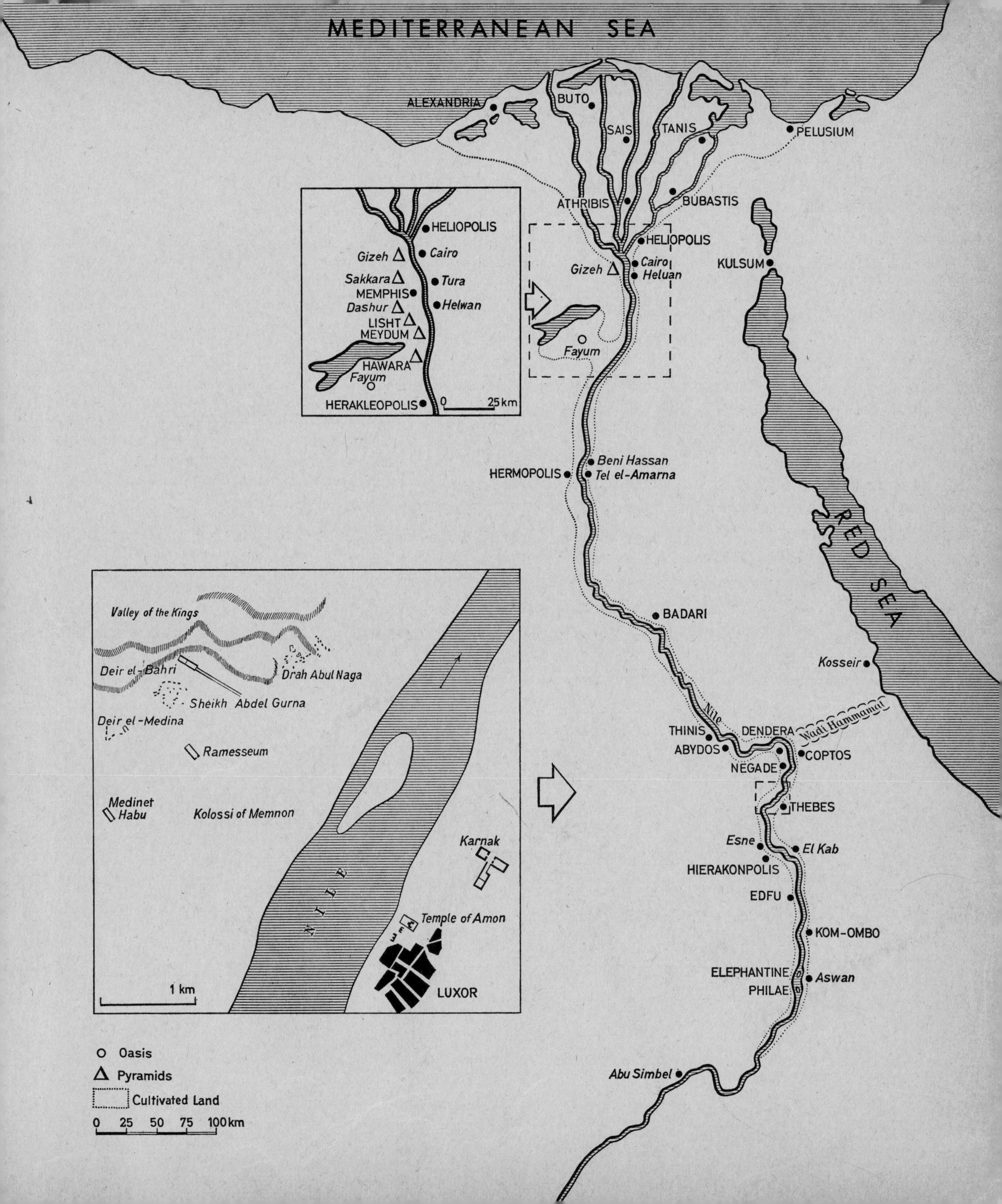

MEDITERRANEAN SEA
ALEXANDRIA
BUTO
SAIS
TANIS
PELUSIUM
ATHRIBIS
BUBASTIS
HELIOPOLIS
Gizeh
Cairo
Heluan
KULSUM
Fayum
HELIOPOLIS
Gizeh
Cairo
Sakkara
Tura
MEMPHIS
Dashur
Helwan
LISHT
MEYDUM
HAWARA
Fayum
HERAKLEOPOLIS
0
25 km
Beni Hassan
HERMOPOLIS
Tel el-Amarna
RED SEA
BADARI
Kosseir
Nile
Wadi Hammamat
THINIS
DENDERA
ABYDOS
COPTOS
NEGADE
THEBES
Esne
El Kab
HIERAKONPOLIS
EDFU
KOM-OMBO
ELEPHANTINE
Aswan
PHILAE
Abu Simbel
Valley of the Kings
Deir el-Bahri
Drah Abul Naga
Sheikh Abdel Gurna
Deir el-Medina
Ramesseum
Medinet Habu
Kolossi of Memnon
Karnak
NILE
Temple of Amon
LUXOR
1 km
Oasis
Pyramids
Cultivated Land
0 25 50 75 100km

Among the Greeks, in the Old as in the New Testament and later throughout the whole sphere of European culture man occupies a special position. Nature was created to serve him. The human being is the crown of Creation.

The preaceful presence of the whole animal kingdom in Paradise at the time of the creation of man is accepted as a given fact. The question whether, after the Fall, the animals also lost their right to the Garden of Eden as a result of Lucifer taking the shape of a serpent did not particularly concern the Western world. In its notion of the celestial Paradise, to which the human soul may attain, the soulless animal has no place. Among the Greeks, to name only one example, the eagle has access to

Nature and man

Olympus as the attribute of Zeus. In the Christian faith animals usually enter heaven only as symbols—the Lamb of God, the dove in the nimbus that stands for the Holy Ghost. We find vestiges of the old nature religion in goat-footed Pan and the Devil's horse's hoof.

In the East and particularly in Egypt no such division ever took place. Man remains a natural being, forming a unity with animals and plants and is still related to nature even after his death. The magnificence of the portrayals of animals is partly due to this interrelationship.

Depictions of a religious character of man-animals or animal-men fall within the same domain of ideas. In the sphinx we have the human head combined with the body of a lion, i. e. the highest power of the spirit coupled with the greatest strength of the animal. It became an embodiment of the rising sun, of the struggle against the powers of darkness, of the affirmation of day, of new life. Contrary to the Egyptian sphinx, the Greek sphinx is female. The Hittites had seen the representations of standing winged bulls at Dur-Sargon in Assyria. The sphinxes were created as gate-figures at Alaca Höyük after contact with the Egyptians.

Combination of the two elements gave rise to the new from with a female torso and a typically

ancient-Egyptian hair style, in a standing position and with side wings. The female sphinx reached Hellas via the mainlaind of Asia Minor. From then on, the emphasis was on the mythological and enigmatic element. Whereas recollection of the myths of centaurs and mermaids provide a certain basis for the understand ing of such figures, modern man finds totally alien the combination of animal head and human body such as we see, for example, in the Cretan minotaur.
In Egypt certain animals appear to be superior to man. The ibis, whose arrival at a particular season unfailingly heralded the new waters of the rising Nile, became the ibis-headed Thoth, the divine scribe. The mountain hawk of Upper Egypt, which not even the swiftest arrow could reach, which dropped like a bolt from the clear sky, never missed its prey and soared aloft again in equally vertical flight till it was lost to the eye, became Horus, the distant one, who comes from the distance and flies back into the distance. These few examples may suffice to give an idea of the specific character of these half human, half animal figures. Cruelty, or even mere indifference towards animals was unknown in ancient Egypt. Even portrayals of sacrificial victims are entirely objective and show no pleasure in suffering. When the joys of the chase are represented in pictures of hunting, we find evidence of intimate and humane observation placed alongside the hunted or slain game, such as a bird's nest with eggs, butterflies disporting themselves, or chicks rescued by the hand of a child. Not for nothing is the hieroglyph for "CHILD" a chick.

Every civilization represents a stage in man's evolution, and in its time and within its geographical area the Egyptian civilization was astonishingly advanced.
In Egyptian painting, the landscape lacked the interconnection between natural phenomena. It consisted rather of a simple juxtaposition of individual elements, of water and earth, flower, bush and tree. Greek art, and Roman art after it, introduced the representation of space into landscape painting. No original Greek fresco painting has come down to us, but the mosaics bear witness to the mastery of perspective; landscapes served the purpose of a background to the myths of gods and heroes, and occasionally also to the lives of ordinary men. Mountains and groves are drawn into the battles of the giants as they are into idylls. Nature on its own is rarely observed, described or depicted.
The land of Egypt with its single river, paucity of trees, bare rocks and endless deserts is grudging and harsh. Yet to the nomads, hunters, herdsmen, peasants and even to the city-dwellers it remained the source of all life. Earth, water and tree were the dwellings of nature's deities. All the more astonishing, therefore is the fact that when he looked at Nature the Egyptian could put aside all religious and utilitarian contacts with it and forget himself in contemplative appreciation of its beauty.
In the poem *Argument of a Man Tired of Life with his Soul* the poet describes this man's state of mind to a landscape after rain. In his *Ode to the Sun* Akhenaton speaks of Nature waiting fearfully in the darkness for the awakening sun. The ceiling of a tomb is painted with branches and creepers full of singing-birds, locusts, butterflies and crickets. This has nothing to do either with religious symbolism or with the idea of game to be hunted on the way to the Next World. This pictorial imagery, unusual in a tomb, is not fortuitous, but evidence that the nature-loving occupant believed that this same sight would continue to delight him in the Next World.

TREES. Sycamores, dates and doum palms. On the date palm are two stalks from which the clusters of dates have been cut. Water is always rendered as seen from above. The fishbone pattern represents the ripples on the surface during a light breeze. (Senedjem, Tomb No. 1, 19 Dyn., Deir el-Medina.)

Doum Palms. The dead Pashedu is drinking from the waters of the Amentit. The inscription reads: to be transformed into a palm tree in order to drink from the waters of the Amentit. The superimposition of the tree trunk on the human body is not to be interpreted as perspective, but rather as the symbolic representation of the wish to change into a tree. The ornamental shape of the palm leaves is noteworthy. The annual rings on the trunk are represented by the severed leaf-ribs. The hatching on the outline of the trunk represents the fibrous palm bast. (Tomb No. 345, 20. Dyn., Deir el-Medina.)

Doum Palms at Karnak. In the background Nectanebo's pylon. (361–343 b. c., 30 Dyn.)

Picking Dates. (Rekhmare, Tomb No. 100, 18 Dyn., Sheikh Abdel Gurna.)

Date Palms and Pylon. Date palms in front of the pylon of Evergertus I Ptolemaeus. (238 B. C., southern enclosure-wall at Karnak.)

Goslings and Doves. The curious practice of rendering details with great precision against a background of large areas and forms produces an admirable unity. (Tomb of Ptah-hotep, Sakkara, 5 Dyn., Old Kingdom.)

Swallow. Although the bird is part of an inscription it constitutes, with its compact outline and modelling, an independent, lifelike artistic creation. (Outer wall, Great Temple, Karnak, New Kingdom.)

Duck. This relief is likewise not a separate representation of a duck, but part of an inscription. Ramses II usurped the works of his predecessors by chiselling away their names. To escape a similar fate, his inscriptions had to be cut very deep. The hieroglyph "duck" becomes an insolently strutting bird. (Great Temple, Karnak, 20 Dyn.)

Owl. The almost human expression of the owl's head is in strange contrast to the schematic outline and graphically simplified legs. Traces of paint. Here too part of an inscription. (Great Temple, Karnak, 20 Dyn., New Kingdom.)

Swan and Geese. The centre of the picture is occupied by the erect heads of the geese. To break the monotonous sequence of the birds, the head on the right is thrust forward towards the edge of the picture. The impression of attack and flight is intensified by its parallelism with the aggresive swan's head on the left. (Tomb of Ptah-hotep, Sakkara, 5 Dyn., Old Kingdom.)

SILK HERONS. A single silk heron of such perfect poise and balance would have been a work of art in itself. The multiplication of the figure, which could have led to monotonous repetition, becomes here a magnificent intensification. Behind the four almost identical herons stands a fifth with open beak pointing in the opposite direction. For stylistic reasons its legs have been omitted. (Tomb of Ptah-hotep, Sakkara, 5. Dyn.)

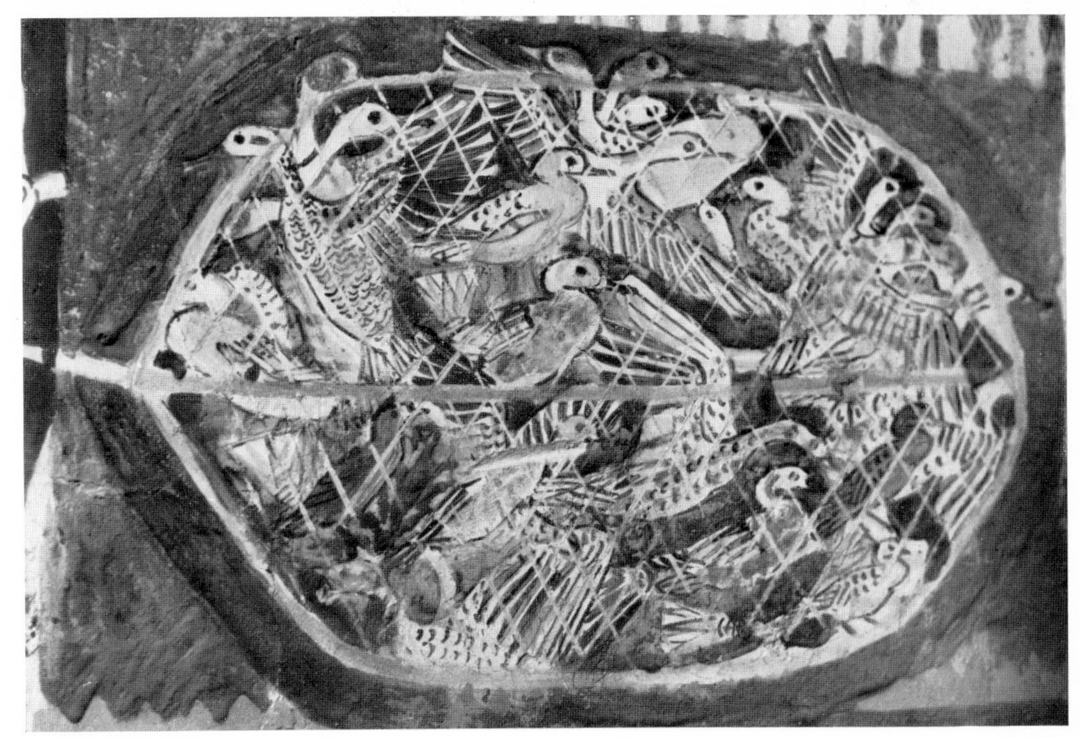

Duck-Catching. Frightened by the fallen clap-net, the ducks and wild geese still free are fluttering up into the air. Those caught in the nets seem already to have abandoned themselves to their fate. (Tomb of Ptah-hotep, Sakkara, 5 Dyn.)

Ducks in the Clap-net. This painting executed more than 1200 years later is in marked contrast to the disciplined austerity of the relief above. The meshes of the net form an orderly ornamental pattern over the wriggling confusion of projecting heads and out-spread, wildly beating wings. (Tomb No. 52, Nakht, 18 Dyn., Sheikh Abdel Gurna.)

Hauling in the Clap-nets. The upper row of men have fallen over backwards because the rope has broken. In the lower row, one man is looking in the opposite direction, thus breaking up the orderly arrangement of men engaged in a common task. (Tomp of Ptah-hotep, Sakkara, 5 Dyn.)

Carrier Running. Young pigeons and wild ducks being transferred in cages. (Tomb of Ptah-hotep, Sakkara, 5 Dyn.)

Wild Geese in a Cage. Captured wild geese are being put in cages, here represented by a simple rectangle without bars. The crossed hands hold the struggling goose's beating wings in check. (Tomb of Ptah-hotep, Sakkara, 5 Dyn.)

FISHING TACKLE. Fish-hooks, harpoons for catching hippopotami, nets and stone weights for dragnets. (Old and Middle Kingdom, Cairo Museum.)

FISHERMAN WITH HIS CATCH. This figure is a detail from a scene showing the presentation of offerings The drawing of the Nile fish is entirely true to life, whereas proportions, because the fish are offerings, are consciously exaggerated. (Tomb of Mehu, Sakkara, 5–6 Dyn.)

CATCHING FISH WITH A DRAGNET. The dragnet is being pulled along between two reed boats.
The model illustrating everyday activities shown on the right is of wood coated with stucco and painted. It is a tomb offering of the type which, in its detailed execution, occurs chiefly in the Middle Kingdom. (Tomb of Mehenket-ure, Middle Kingdom, Cairo Museum.)

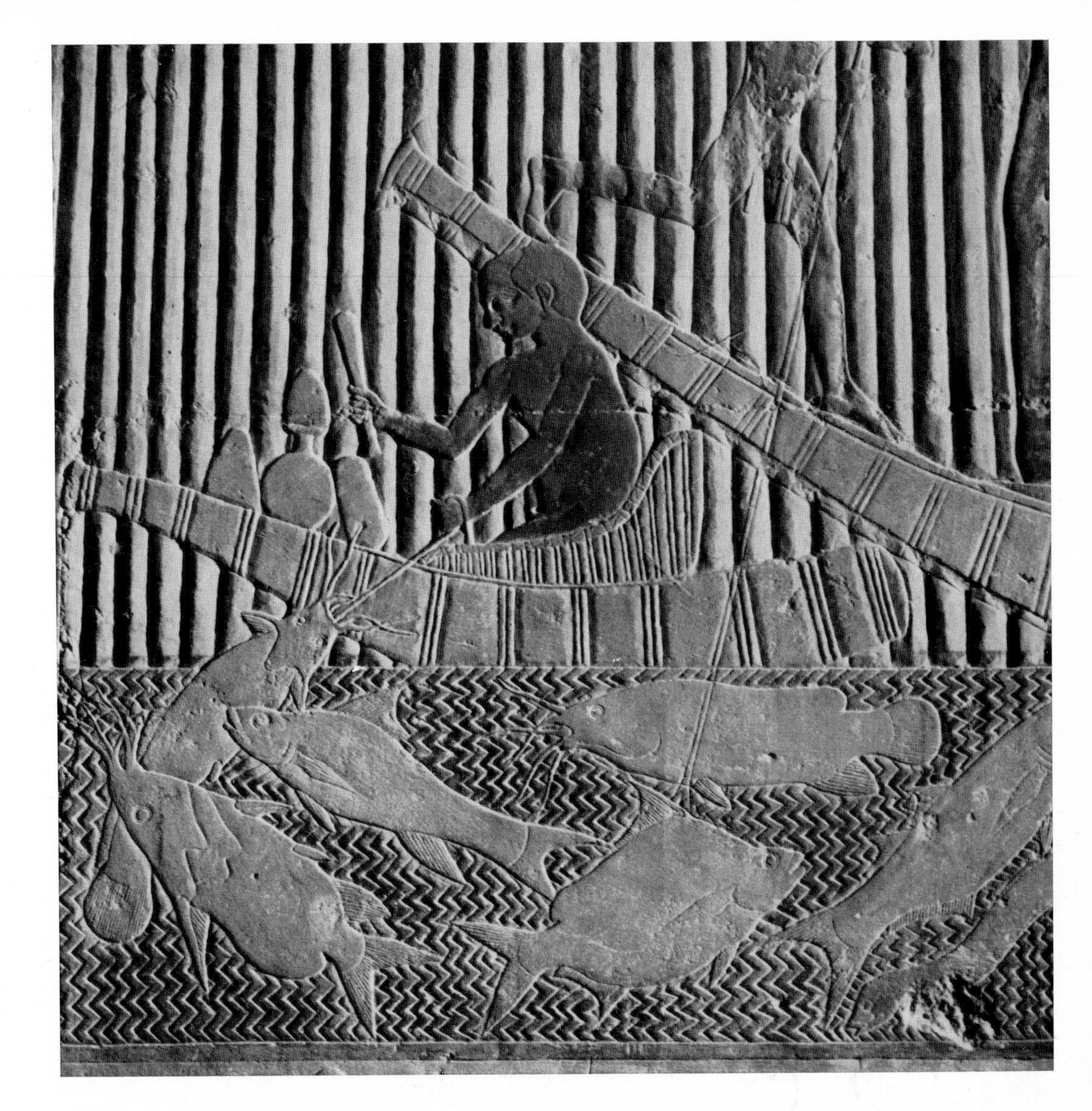

Fishermen with Lines. The background consists of a papyrus thicket of which only the stems are visible. The little reed boat has a seat resembling a basket chair. The fisherman is stunning the fish he has caught with a club. The realistic rendering makes it quite easy to identify the fish among the Nile fauna. Bottom right, an eel. (Tomb of Ti, Sakkara, 5 Dyn.)

ANUBIS (sculpture). In its sovereign nobility the animal's head, silently waiting, looks astoundingly lifelike. Painted wood, inlaid eyes. Interior of the ears, collar and ribbon are lined with gold leaf. (Treasure of Tut-ankh-Amon, 18 Dyn., Cairo Museum.)

ANUBIS. The jackal-dog Anubis personifies the guardians of the dead. The wedge-shaped head, the elongated human eye and the white line of the mouth with the two end dots combine to create an uncanny impression of a beast alert and ready to spring. With its free decorative background the painting looks extraordinarily modern. (Tomb No. 1, Senedjem, 20 Dyn., Deir-el-Medina.)

CAT. These very beautiful sculptures of cats made of bronze or wood were containers for mummified cats. Noteworthy is the stress on the almost geometrical circle of the shoulder, which breaks and then unites the line from the neck to the curve of the back. The hole behind the ear was intended for a gold ring. (Saïte period, Cairo Museum.)

GIRAFFE. Giraffes were popular as gifts presented by tributary princes from the south. The monkey on the giraffe's neck is a subsequent addition of the painter's. (Tomb No. 100, Rekhmare, 18 Dyn., Sheikh Abdel Gurna.)

HORSE. The horses were relatively small, thickset and wore trimmed manes. They entered the country from the East around 1700 B. C. along with the invading Hyksos. (Tomb No. 56, Usirhat, 18 Din., Sheikh Abdel Gurna.)

Gazelle Hunting. This detail shows animals racing wildly away in all directions. Even in the case of the dying gazelle the line of neck and back, drawn in a single stroke, conveys the movement of flight. (Tomb No. 56, Usirhat, 18 Dyn., Sheikh Abdel Gurna.)

Hunting Dog. Thoroughbred dogs were man's indispensable companions while hunting. The whole composition of this dog leads from its long, sinewy legs, through the slender loins and massive shoulders to the powerful neck and pointed muzzle and sums up the implacable spirit of the chase. (Tomb of Mereruka, 5 Dyn., Sakkara.)

MARKET THIEF. The baboon standing on its hind legs is holding on to a thief. As a badge of office, the guard is carrying a staff topped by an open hand. Anecdotal elements enter into Egyptian art more often than is generally supposed. (From Sakkara, 6 Dyn., Cairo Museum.)

The seasons (Agriculture)

Egypt, an almost rainless country stretching along the banks of a river and surrounded by deserts, had no agricultural land apart from the narrow strips bordering the Nile. In ancient times the delta was a vast area of marsh habitable only on the edges and on the east side. The plague of flies in these regions must have been exceptionally intense, since it was specifically referred to in the instructions written by King Akhthoes (Ninth Dynasty, 2100–2070 B. C.) for his son Phiops. He speaks with regret of the shepherd whom the flies almost killed when he had to travel to Lower Egypt to fetch the purchase-money for his flocks. When the Nile rose in the summer the neighbouring fields or whole tracts of land, according to how high it rose, were submerged.

Of the heavenly bodies the stars, with the exception of Sirius, had no religious significance, whereas the sun and moon had a very special one. Furthermore the sun was important in determining the length of the year. The star Sirius, after a long absence, reappeared in the Egyptian sky in high summer. Simultaneously, the long-awaited rising of the Nile took place. The beginning of the year was reckoned by the conjunction of these two natural phenomena.

Immediately before the longed-for floods, the ibis came into the country from the south, as though to herald them. If it failed to arrive, the population had to reckon with a dry year. The bird became the good messenger, acquainted with the will of the gods. Finally it was venerated as the attribute of the All-Knowing One. The god Thoth was born, a human-figure with the head of an ibis and a style and writing-tablet in his hands. The present-day university of Cairo bears Thoth in its badge.

To return to the seasons. The Egyptian calendar, unlike that of other peoples' of the time, contained twelve months of thirty days each, that is to say three hundred and sixty days. To make it tally with the solar year the necessary number of extra days were added and declared holidays.

In accordance with the climate of the country, the year was divided into Flood, Sowing and Harvest, that is to say into three seasons and not into four as is the case elsewhere. Sowing and harvest relate to the various kinds of corn, the country's staple food.

On the higher, terraced fields vegetables and fruit flourished the whole year round. They were irrigated by a widely ramified network of canals. Their upkeep and the just distribution of the water called for a vigilant administration. As already stated in the Introduction, diverting water from a neighbour's fields was one of the sins for which the soul had to answer before the Supreme Judge. The State tax consisted mainly in the delivery of a percentage of the corn harvest.

Vast storage chambers were built to accommodate the considerable quantities of grain paid over as tax. In years of drought they proved themselves a wise precaution on the part of the State. In addition, supplies were needed for the Army, for the outposts of the defence forces situated in the desert, and not least for all those who could not engage in agriculture: the castes of priests and scribes.

The scribes were responsible for the registration of water rights, corn tax, the storage and distribution of the State stocks. In the scribe class we have the origin of the civil servant.

PLOUGHING AND SOWING. Senedjem at the wooden plough, behind him his wife Igne-fert sowing. The wall-painting represents agriculture in Yaru, the Next World. Hence the man portrayed is called the "servant in the place of freedom". (Tomb No. 1, Senedjem, 20 Dyn., Deir-el-Medina.)

Surveyor. Ripe fields were measured before the harvest to ascertain the length of the field and the height of the corn for purposes of the water tax. The blind surveyor is being led by a boy upon whose head he is resting his hand. (Tomb No. 69, Mena, 18 Dyn., Sheikh Abdel Gurna.)

Reaping. The man is reaping the enormous ears of corn with a sickle, while the woman gathers them up into a basket. In the Next World, where all effort is removed from everything, grain grows to three times its normal size. (Tomb No. 1, Senedjem, 10 Dyn., Deir el-Medina.)

SHEAVES. Three men gathering up sheaves. The curious thing about these sheaves is that the ears are placed at alternate ends, with the result that they become interlocked and do not require binding. (Tomb of Ti, Sakkara, 5 Dyn.)

Asses During Threshing. Corn was threshed by driving asses round a threshing floor enclosed by a wall. In order to break up and enliven the row of asses one head is thrust forward. For compositional reasons, the legs of this ass have been consciously omitted. The animals resemble the wild ass more closely than the familiar domestic animal. (Tomb of Ti, Sakkara, 5 Dyn.)

Filling a Bushel. The conical corn measure narrower at the top is similar to the bushel still used in Egypt. On the relief, the grains of corn have only been carved half-way along the heap. (Sarcophagus of second wife of Mentuhotep, 12 Dyn., Cairo Museum.)

SEPARATING CHAFF AND WHEAT. The grains are being thrown up into the air with wooden scoops. The bending girls are sweeping away the chaff left behind. All the workers are wearing headscarves to keep the chaff out of their hair. (Tomb No. 69, Mena, 18 Dyn., Sheikh Abdel Gurna.)

STATE GRANARIES. Granaries from the precincts of the mortuary temple of Ramses II. Of the filling-holes in the roof, the last but one has been preserved in its original state. The iron relieving arches are of modern date. (New Kingdom, 21 Dyn., West Thebes.)

GRANARY OF A HOUSE. Women are emptying the contents of their sacks into the roof-holes of a granary. In the upper right-hand corner sits a scribe registering each entry; lower right by the door a guard, recognizable by his stick. Wooden models of this kind were used in the Middle Kingdom to decorate tombs and to some extent replaced reliefs or paintings. (Middle Kingdom, Cairo Museum.)

Working at the Mortar. Two men and a woman working together at the mortar. Noteworthy is the frontal position of the central figure, rare in Egyptian art. (Limestone relief from Sakkara, 5 Dyn., Cairo Museum.)

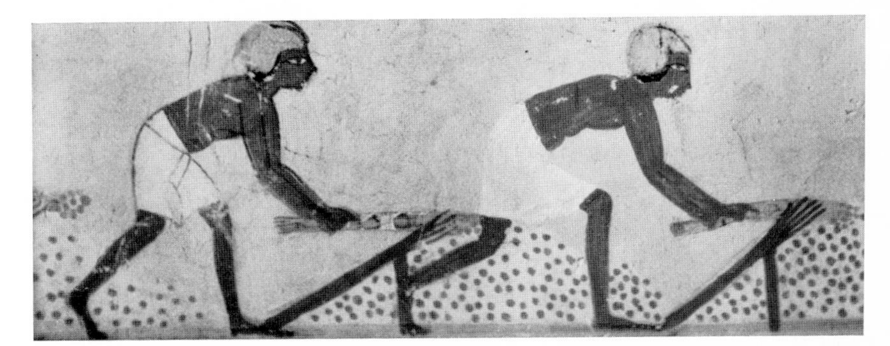

Heaping Grain. Heaped grain is being cleaned and smoothed with hand brooms. The grids placed on the left side of each heap determine the height and slope of the flat cones. (Tomb No. 69, Mena, 18 Dyn., Sheikh Abdel Gurna.)

THE MAID. The inscription on the plinth calls the working woman "ISHA-KET, maid of UR-IR-EN". The calm, noble face explains this unusual case of a servant being named. The activity she is engaged in has been described variously as kneading dough or grinding corn. The former is more likely. (From Sakkara, 5 Dyn., Cairo Museum.)

Handicrafts (Building)

Houses in Neolithic times were built of reed matting daubed with mud. The sun-dried, moulded brick already occurs in the pre-Dynastic period. The technique of brick building as used for larger temples and royal palaces was evolved during the First and Second Dynasty. Both secular and religious edifices were built of brick. Occasionally hewn stone was employed to cover the floors of temples, to line the walls of tombs and for steps and trapdoors. Where the front was of large dimensions, brick building involved a series of projecting rectangular piers and intervening recesses. The same method is also seen in the buildings of ancient Mesopotamia.

In 2850 the brilliant architect Imhotep achieved for King Zoser, Third Dynasty, the first great building of hewn stone: the step pyramid of Sakkara. As a tomb, with the temple precincts surrounding it, this building was religious in character. The important achievements at the beginning of a cultural period do not merely leave a decisive mark upon ensuing ages, but are turned by tradition into inviolable laws. Ever since the erection of the step pyramid, worked stone was credited with a sacred character and regarded as symbolizing eternity. As a result, it became customary to construct secular buildings of unbaked brick. They had to be made of perishable material: houses, like their occupants, were transitory. The theory that stone was the building material of Upper Egypt and mud bricks that of Lower Egypt lacks all foundation in fact, since stone building was evolved in Sakkara, that is to say in Lower Egypt.

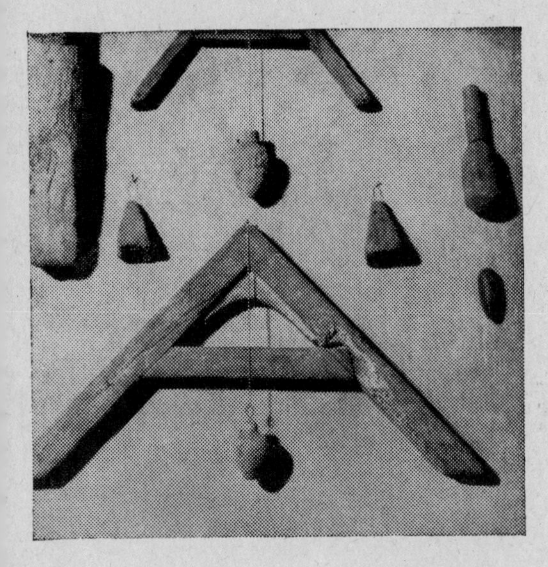

Dwelling houses were built of sun-dried bricks made with a mixture of mud, sand and chopped straw. These bricks were of slightly smaller dimensions than those in general use today. From the earlier dynasties we are acquainted with bricks measuring: $24 \times 10 \times 5$ cm. and $23 \times 12 \times 7$ cm. Unlike stone, sun-dried building material does not conduct heat and hence is very well suited to a climate that is often hot. The bricklayer's trowel was very similar in shape to that used today; the plumb-line and plumb-square took the place of the water-level, while measuring-rods, try-squares, setting-out lines and setting-out pegs were customary tools.

Thin chalk-lines used in surveying and building must be of constant length. In a climate in which intense, dry heat alternates with periods of extreme humidity (while the Nile is in flood) shrinking and stretching must be guarded against. The strands of these cords are often so skilfully interwoven that even a tremendous pull causes no increase in the length. W. B. Emery examined a flax rope about one centimetre thick, dating from archaic times, and found it to be made up of three separate strands, each composed of no less than a hundred and ninety threads.

Whether the houses were of one or more storeys, a flight of steps always led to the flat, slightly inclined roof, which was equipped with gutters. When the roof beams were of some length they were supported by palm trunks, which stood in the room like pillars. The window apertures were narrow and high and protected from wind and sand by gathered and stretched mats. The wooden doors

opened on pivots fitting into bearings in the lintel and threshold. The outer walls were inclined slightly inwards, thus increasing the stability of the buildings, which always stood on soft soil. They were generally plastered inside and out, or if not plastered then at least whitewashed. To smooth off the plaster the craftsman used a thin board with bevelled edges and a firm hand-grip in the centre, about three feet long and six to eight inches wide. On the ceilings and walls we find ornamental paintings as well as more or less realistic depictions of plants and birds. In Tel el-Amarna even painted floors have been preserved.
The fixed fireplace, enclosed by walls on three sides, was situated in the courtyard, that is to say outside the roofed section of the house. In addition, a portable charcoal brazier of fired earthenware with a conical foot was used. Food was grilled or roasted on a spit over the glowing embers.

Stone and Stonemasons

Besides limestone and sandstone, the Egyptians also worked very hard types of stone, such as red and grey granite, black sienite, the strongly veined diorite and others. For smaller vessels and sculptures they also used the extremely hard quartzite and green schist, a very homogeneous volcanic ash that has been subjected to compression for millions of years and is exceptionally hard and brittle. Expeditions were despatched to remote areas to bring certain kinds of stone back to the cities. The most celebrated granite and sienite quarries are at Aswan, others in Sinai and yet others in the mountains west of the Red Sea.

The irregular fracture-surface of a hard stone like diorite was smoothed by covering it with glowing charcoal. When the stone was evenly heated to a certain depth, it was chilled with cold water. The resulting surface-tension produced fine cracks and the broken layer was then worked with handstones, or in later ages with broad-headed bronze hammers. To detach a block of the required dimensions from its parent mass, a line was drawn along the limits and wedge-shaped slots driven into it at regular intervals. The tools used for this were bronze chisels, round wooden mallets and crowbars. Dry wooden wedges were driven into the slots and then soaked with water, particularly at night when evaporation was slight, till the expanding wood split off the block of stone. Great experience was needed to recognize usable blocks of the requisite size in the closed mass of rock and then to detach them. Blocks weighing hundreds of tons and monumental sculptures were transported with the aid of massive sledges drawn by a whole army of men. Any wheel, however broad, would have sunk in the sandy soil and no bronze axle would have stood the strain. If the block was being transported over sand or earth, water was continually poured in front of the runners to make them slide more easily. On stony ground a movable log-road was laid in front of the sledge, which was rolled over it. The logs over which the sledge had passed were taken up and replaced in front of it. The shipping of Queen Hatsheput's obelisk, which still stands in the temple at Karnak, is portrayed in a relief in the temple of Deir el-Bahri.

Felling Trees. The curving groundline on which the tree-feller is kneeling characterizes the landscape as hilly. The important thing is the movement of chopping and its effect—the falling tree. By comparison, the relative proportions of man and tree are unimportant. Branches lie on the ground, an unfelled tree stands on the right above. (Tomb of Nakht, 18 Dyn., Sheikh Abdel Gurna.)

Carpenters. Trimming a tree trunk. The axe-heads are bound into the wooden hafts with thin leather thongs. In the centre the stump of a branch is being cut away with an adze. The men are wearing close-fitting leather caps. (Tomb of Ti, Sakkara, 5 Dyn.)

BUILDING WORKERS. Above: Making sun-dried bricks. The mixture of clay, sand and chaff is placed in the dark wooden mould. Below: The non-Negroid faces of the dark-skinned men with their short, straight noses and pointed beards indicate foreign origin. (Tomb No. 100, Rekhmare, 18 Dyn., Sheikh Abdel Gurna.)

Plumb-Squares. The plumb-square, a forerunner of the water-level, was used to check flat surfaces. On the right a small wooden mallet. Plumb-stones for vertical and horizontal surfaces. (Date uncertain, probably New Kingdom, Cairo Museum.)

Mason. A kneeling workman with a hand-hoe. This tool was used for various purposes, such as hacking up earth, mixing masses of clay, straightening a brick wall etc. The angle of the blade to the handle was determined by the length of the binding. (Tomb No. 100, Rekhmare, 18 Dyn., Sheikh Abdel Gurna.)

Water Carriers. Men of the building team with water vessels. The earthenware jars shaped like amphorae differ from the well-known wine and beer containers by having rounder bases, necks that were shorter and widened out more, and no handles. (Tomb No. 100, Rekhmare, 18 Dyn., Sheikh Abdel Gurna.)

Rear of the Summerhouse. Left: Large unmovable window with light-slits. Centre: Two-winged door with pivot hinges and external crossbar. Above it the fanlight. Right: Outside of a door that can be bolted from inside. (Middle Kingdom, *ca.* 1800 B. C., Cairo Museum.)

SUMMERHOUSE. Model of a summerhouse with trees and pond. The multiple columns clearly show that they were originally made of bundles of palm ribs and reeds bound together. On the edge of the roof three spouts to drain off the rare but violent rainfall. (Middle Kingdom, *ca.* 1800 B. C., Cairo Museum.)

MEASURING RODS. Above: Five-sided measuring instruments. Below: A model measure of stone upon which the wooden measuring rods were gauged. Measure of length: 1 cubit = 20 inches, subdivided into 7 hand's breadths and 28 finger's breadths. (From various periods, Cairo Museum.)

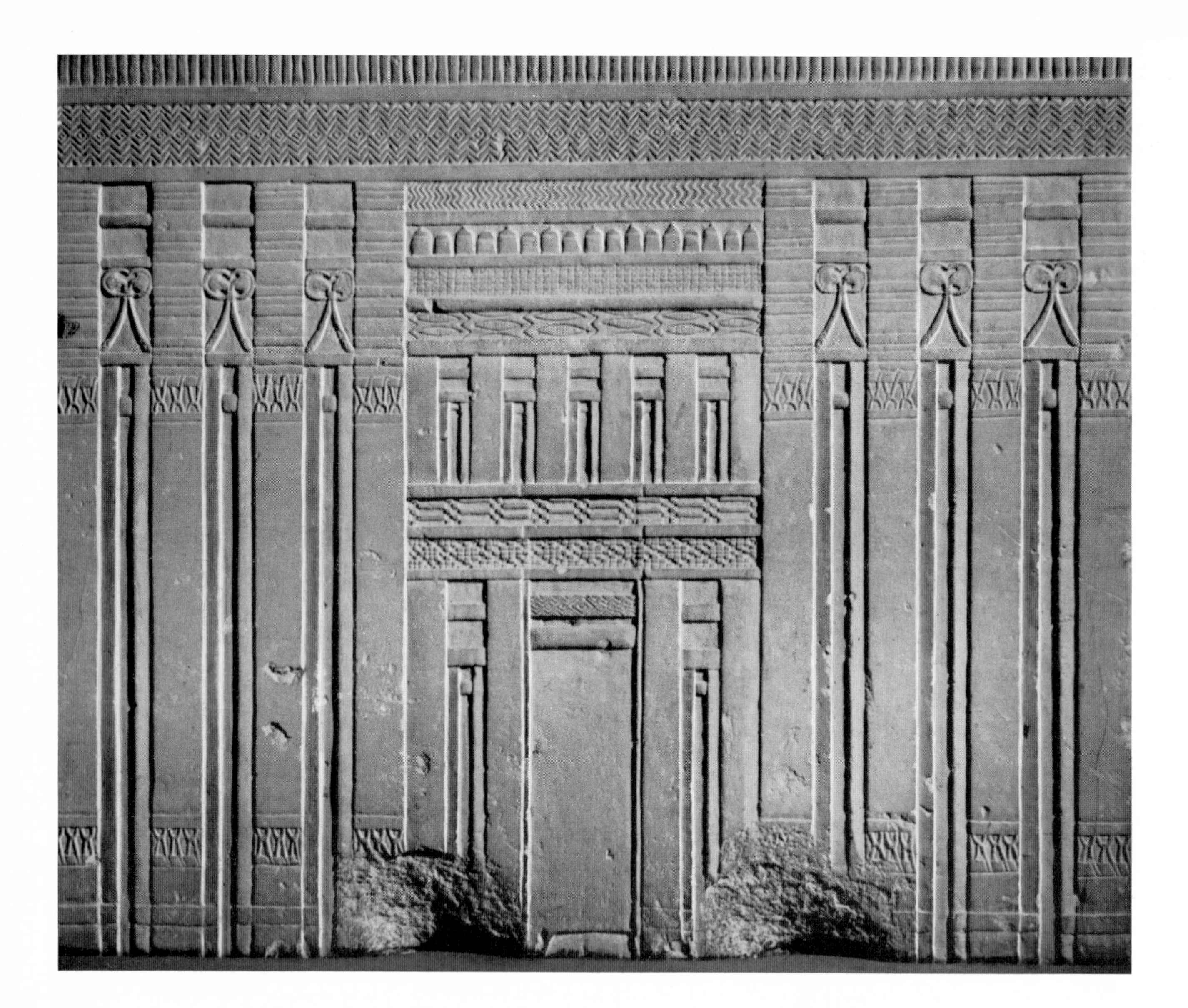

Model of the Front of a House. Over the entrance the bricks have been arranged in various patterns. High narrow windows on either side of the door, shaded by sunblinds. The rope for stretching the mat forming the blind is wound several times round a crossbar at the top and bottom. Above this two bound-up papyrus plants as decoration. (Part of a sarcophagus, Old Kingdom, Cairo Museum.)

Marking Cords. For marking out plots of ground, such as agricultural holdings or building sites. Above: A crowbar. Left: An axe-shaped chisel. Below: Stone plumb-weights. (Date uncertain, Cairo Museum.)

Model of a Joiner's Workshop. Left: Squaring a piece of timber. Centre: Sawing a plank. Right: Gouging out grooves. The rectangular box is a sarcophagus. Behind: Smoothing a sheet of timber with handstones and sand powder. (Middle Kingdom, *ca.* 1800 B. C., Cairo Museum.)

Woodworking. Sawing an upright log. The stone hanging on the rod prevents the saw from jamming. Next to this, gouging out grooves. (Tomb of Ti, Sakkara, 5 Dyn.)

Boatbuilding. Shaping the bow of a ship with short adzes. This tool was the forerunner of the plane. (Tomb of Ti, Sakkara, 5 Dyn.)

WHEELMAKERS. Finishing a wheel with the adze. Compared with this picture from the New Kingdom, the one below from the Old Kingdom shows the change in style that had taken place over some 1300 years. (Chapel of Min from Sakkara, New Kingdom, Cairo Museum.)

CARPENTERS. Two carpenters smoothing a table-top with flattened handstone and fine sand powder. Beside them a third is using a handborer. The headrest lying under the table was used as a pillow; similar wooden pillows are still employed in Japan. (Tomb of Ti, Sakkara, 5 Dyn.)

Relief with Guidelines. Thin guidelines are visible above and on the right-hand side. By the head down to the shoulder they are close together to show the intervals between the forehead, eye, nose, mouth and chin. By the body the spaces between the lines are seven times as large. Even when a complete grid of squares is formed, this did not serve the purpose of transferring a working sketch, but was an aid to preserving the traditional canon of proportions. (Stele of Memi, First Intermediate Period, Cairo Museum.)

STONECARVERS. Left: Chiselling a statue. The finer chisels are fitted into wooden handles. The mallets are club-shaped. Right: Polishing the statue with specially cut, very hard handstones. (From Sakkara, 5 Dyn., Cairo Museum.)

The designation for a sculptor was "the enlivener." His tools included chisels of various shapes and degrees of hardness; polishing was done with sand and oval handstones. Mirror-smooth surfaces were obtained with the aid of quartz powder, leather and water. Woodcarvings were usually coated with stucco and painted and, as with limestone carvings, the original paint may frequently be seen today. Harder types of stone were only partially painted, eyes and eyebrows being picked out with a dark colour. Death masks and their gypsum moulds were already made in the Old Kingdom; the casts were worked over and used for the *Ka* statues. Many of these masks from the Akhenaton period have been preserved, all of them taken from the living model. Since they are all confined to the facial area, and never render the whole head in the round, they must be looked upon as aids to the production of portrait statues. Masks were not used in ancient Egypt. While embalming, the priest, as the representative of Anubis, wore on his shoulders a wide earthenware head with the features of Anubis, but not a mask.

An Unfinished Statue. In its unfinished state, this statue comes close to our contemporary taste. Work on this statue of a pharaoh, whose dignity is shown by the uraeus on his brow, was probably abandoned because the hands bearing the offering broke off while they were being chiselled. (Black sienite, Cairo Museum.)

Chasers and Sculptors. In the centre and left: Chasing metal vessels. Right: The statue is probably hollow cast. If it were of stone or solid metal, the worker could never maintain this position, and also the working plinth would be too weak. (Chapel of Min from Sakkara, New Kingdom, Cairo Museum.)

Chisels. A selection of stonecarvers' chisels of various shapes. In the centre a fine sculptor's chisel. Extreme right: Two bronze wedges. (Date uncertain, Cairo Museum.)

Temple of Khonsu. This temple from the Late period contains one of the few windows still perfectly preserved. The light-slits are chiselled out of a granite slab and not left free in a frame that has been fitted together. (Temple precinct, Karnak.)

Our knowledge of Egyptian food is chiefly derived from portrayals of offerings, from the desiccated remains in bowls and other vessels (food for the journey of the soul) inside tombs, or from the offerings left by visitors in the anteroom of the tomb. These consist of various kinds of cereal and fruit. Of the remnants of liquids found, one has been identified with certainty as milk.

The funerary figures of earthenware or stone dating from the Old Kingdom, the forerunners of the later *ushabtis*, saw to the welfare of the deceased on his long journey to the Next World by performing their various symbolic functions, such as grinding corn, kneading dough, baking bread,

Food and drink

brewing beer and killing ducks, geese and calves. We are acquainted with whole groups of such figurines of servants dating from the Middle Kingdom. They are of wood coated with stucco and carefully painted. They work in rows, as it were hand in hand. The duck is roasted on a long hand-spit over the charcoal brazier. The cook concerned fans his fire with a fan.

In addition, we are familiar with sequences of wall-paintings and reliefs from the New Kingdom depicting eating and drinking. Where the scene is one of a banquet or festivity, it naturally includes musicians and dancing-girls. The description of the dancing-girl (in Professor J. Spiegel's translation) as "well nourished and of a friendly heart" requires no further comment. Eating at a common table was unknown. Round portable tables on one leg were set before each individual. At table, a ewer and a basin for rinsing the mouth generally stood under or beside the diner's chair. The water contained a disinfectant salt. The drinking-bowls were replenished from jugs. A list of provisions supplied to workmen includes beer as a daily drink. Wine jars have been found bearing inscriptions and seals showing the origin of their contents. Similarly mention is made of how often the wine was drawn off and poured into a fresh jar to prevent it from turning sour.

Grapes are almost invariably shown as dark-blue and only very rarely in shades of yellowish-green. In the way of fruit we find, apart from figs, pomegranates, grapes, the fruit of the baobab and many varieties of dates. Other fruits portrayed have not yet been identified with certainty.

The diet further included vegetables in the shape of several sorts of pumpkins and cucumbers, leguminous plants, long-leaved lettuces, onions and leeks. Fowl included quails, pigeons, ducks and geese. As domestic animals, they were frequently subjected to a fattening process. Chickens first appear in Graeco-Roman times. The chief meats were ibex, sheep, all kinds of cattle and, as a delicacy, gazelle.

Although pigs were kept, their flesh was considered unclean. On the other hand, they could be given as offerings. The poorer people, who could not afford offerings of animals, used to satisfy their religious obligations by leaving behind in temples of pilgrimage small votive figurines of earthenware representing human beings bound. Around the great temple cities fish were permitted as offerings, but for long periods the eating of fish was frowned upon. Yet fishing was a very widespread industry. In regions where it was difficult or impossible to keep animals, as for example round Lake Fayûm, in the Nile delta and on the shores of the Red Sea, fish either fresh or salted must undoubtedly have been an important item of diet.

From pictures and loaves that have been preserved we know that the Egyptians baked bread of many kinds and in many shapes. The variations did not consist merely in the use and blending of various kinds of cereal, but also in the degree of fineness or coarseness to which the flour was ground and in the preparation of dough plain or sweetened with honey. Egyptologists have listed up to forty sorts of bread. Apart from the more or less flat round cake, a conical loaf is known from the Old and Middle Kingdom. The baker heated the conical baking-moulds of earthenware over an open fire till they reached the maximum temperature. Then he coated the inside with a thin layer of dough; the dough was baked in the hot mould without being put back on the fire. This method ensured that it would neither burn nor remain unbaked.

Fatness was never regarded in ancient Egypt as a sign of prosperity. On the contrary it was despised as an indication of intemperance and hence of foolishness. Exceptions to this are known from the time of the New Kingdom. The tendency to moderation was disregarded where drinking was concerned, especially in public taverns. Gardiner refers in the *Bibliotheca aegyptica*, Brussels, to a teacher who reproaches a neglectful pupil. "I have heard that thou forsakest the papyri and givest thyself up to dancing. Thou goest from tavern to tavern, the smell of beer marketh thy path. Men avoid thee when thou staggerest through the streets. Couldst thou forget drink and realize that drunkenness maketh unworthy. Thou deniest thy spirit."

OFFERINGS. This wall-painting has been described as a precursor of the still-life. The objects are shown one above the other in profile, but in reality they are placed side by side. From below upwards: Table top of alabaster, baskets of grapes, in between sweetened loaves, pumpkin, calf's head and leg, tied lettuce leaves, basket of figs, millet, grapes, pumpkin, duck's eggs, crowned with a bunch of lotus flowers. (Tomb of Nakht, 18 Dyn., Sheikh Abdel Gurna.)

Fishes. Particularly striking here is the mingling of side view and view from above. The fish are conceived of as lying flat on their sides, but in order to give a better picture of them are portrayed from a bird's eye view. The platter on the other hand, being in itself unimportant, is shown in profile. (Tomb No. 69, Mena, 18 Dyn., Sheikh Abdel Gurna.)

Shopping Baskets and Bag. Left: Two baskets woven from bast and the leaves of young palm shoots. Right: An open basket, between two loaves a vessel with a lid. (Tomb of Mereruka, Sakkara, 6 Dyn.)

DEAD WILD GOOSE. The plumage has been drawn in the traditional manner. Despite the use of earth colours, the neck with its dead feathers and the closed eyelid have the airy transparency of a watercolour. (Tomb No. 69, Mena, 18 Dyn., Sheikh Abdel Gurna.)

DRAWING AND PLUCKING FOWLS. Noteworthy are the handy sloping board, well adapted to the task, and the stool with the hollowed-out seat. (Tomb No. 52, Nakht, 18 Dyn., Sheikh Abdel Gurna.)

DUCKS ON THE OFFERING TABLE. Preliminary drawing in black and white for a wallpainting on limestone in a deep subterranean tomb-shaft. This brilliant composition with its strict lineation could only have been produced in the Old Kingdom. (Tomb of Mereruka, Sakkara, 6 Dyn.)

OFFERINGS. In a reverently bent posture bringers of offerings carry weightless shoulders of meat. The repetition of the figures intensifies the impression of humility. (Tomb of Mehou, Sakkara, 6 Dyn., discovered by Zaki Saad.)

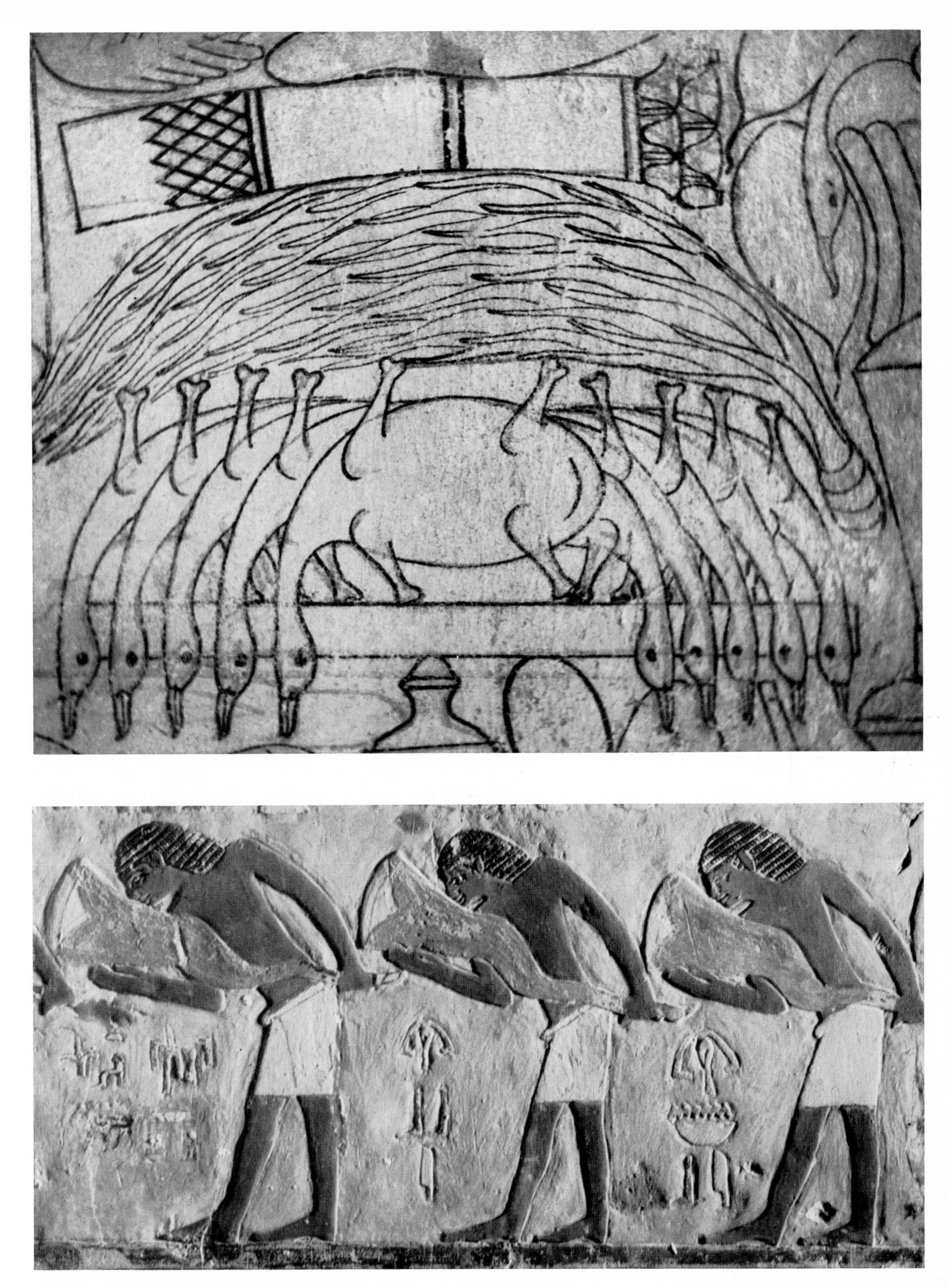

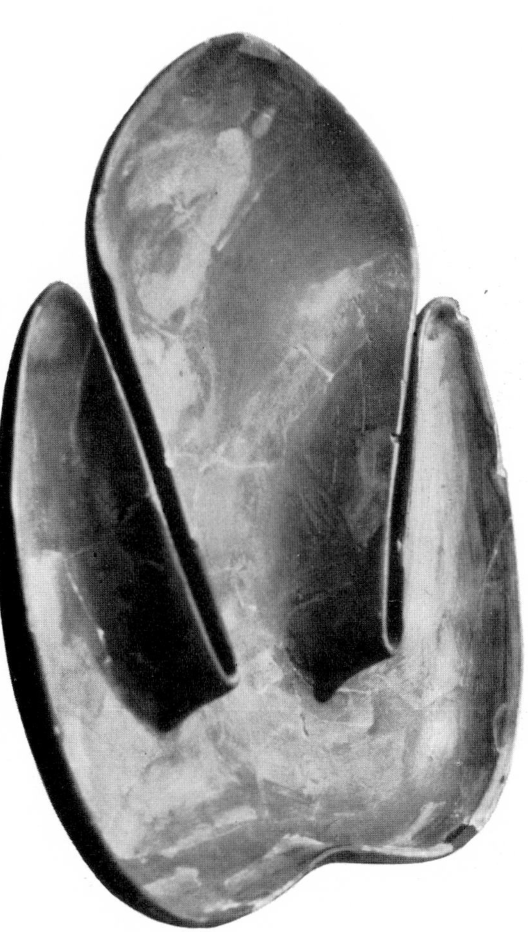

Sieve. Alabaster sieve with handle and raised edge. (Tomb of Tut-ankh-Amon, 18 Dyn., Cairo Museum.)

Earthenware Vessels. Brick-red vessels of fired clay. The very finely ground and sieved clay is so evenly fired that the vessels are almost watertight even without a glaze. The shapes indicate provenance in the early period of the Old Kingdom. Upper right: A jug with a handle in the Cretan style. (Old Kingdom, Cairo Museum.)

Bowls. An alabaster bowl carved in concentric circles. Behind it a square bowl with concave sides of yellow quartzite. (1 Dyn., Sakkara, Cairo Museum.)

Fig-leaf Bowl and Basket. A stylized fig leaf as a bowl. The smaller bowl retains the character of its material even though it has been carved to resemble a woven basket. Both objects carved out of black schist. (Figleaf bowl, mid-1 Dyn.; basket, 2 Dyn.; Cairo Museum.)

COVERED BOWLS. Food offerings other than fruit and field-produce were presented in covered bowls. (Tomb No. 69, Mena, 18 Dyn., Sheikh Abdel Gurna.)

BAKER. Sitting in front of his oven. The earthenware moulds set on it were heated to great intensity and the dough laid in them without being replaced on the fire. The bread was baked in the cooling moulds with no risk of burning. (4–5 Dyn., Cairo Museum.)

POMEGRANATES AND WILD DUCK. The first bearer is carrying in his right hand a bowl of grapes, in his left pomegranates tied into a string. The second has living wild duck suspended from his carrying pole. (Tomb No. 69, Mena, Sheikh Abdel Gurna.)

SERVANT WASHING A JUG. Even the sculpture of an anonymous servant shows the classical style of the Old Kingdom in all its purity. The forms of the body with its relatively small head and broad shoulders are combined in masterly fashion with that of the jug. (Sakkara, 5–6 Dyn., Cairo Museum.)

MAID MAKING BEER. The strenuous work is rendered almost realistically evident through the thrusting arms and the pressure in the back. The entirely indifferent expression of the face is in keeping with the habitual nature of the activity. (Sakkara, 4 Dyn., Cairo Museum.)

EATING. One of Akhenaton's daughters eating. Preliminary drawing for a limestone relief. Slight corrections to the chin and the left hand may be seen. The sculptor's work was not terminated by the cracking of the slab. (Mirit-Aton?, 18 Dyn., Cairo Museum.)

Offering Fruit. The wife offers her husband grapes and cakes on a mat of woven reeds. (Tomb No. 96, Senefer, 18 Dyn., Sheikh Abdel Gurna.)

Vines. The movement of the trailing vines, which cover the whole ceiling, is intensified by the irregularly hewn rock. The circular shapes broken up by three lines represent the vine leaves. (Tomb No. 96, Senefer, 18 Dyn., Sheikh Abdel Gurna.)

TREADING GRAPES. Five boys are treading grapes in a walled trough, holding on to date stalks. The juice is flowing out through a pipe into a low vessel that is being looked after by a sixth boy. Above his head is a row of jars. As may be seen from the vine shoot on the right, this picture is a continuation of the next.

Picking Grapes. In contradistinction to the usual upright vines, we have here the more rarely portrayed vine arbour. The green (copper oxide) of the leaves has faded greatly. The juxtaposition of the heads of fair, straight hair and black curly hair adds a humorous touch. (Both pictures from Tomb No. 52, Nakht, 18 Dyn., Sheikh Abdel Gurna.)

THE DRINK. Senefer's wife is handing her husband a drink. Great care has been lavished upon the interplay of the giving and receiving hands. Arms and hands are heavily outlined, nostrils and lips by contrast are drawn with extremely fine lines. (Tomb No. 96, Senefer, 8 Dyn., Sheikh Abdel Gurna.)

Dress and the toilet

Portrayals of the people who lived in Egypt during the Neolithic period on various vases and in a single wall-painting from Kom el-Akhmar, the second Negada Culture, show no sign of clothing. Yet fragments of cloth, in which idol-like figures were wrapped, have come down to us from this period. On his unguent palette King Narmer, circa 3200 BC, the founder of the ancient Egyptian kingdom, is already portrayed with the loincloth crossed over in front. This article of dress remained essentially unchanged until into the Roman era. The Cairo Museum possesses a large collection of decorated spindle heads of wood and bone dating from pre-Dynastic times. According to W. B. Emery, an examination of the extremely delicate wrapping round the arm of the mummy from the tomb of the pharaoh Djer or Zer (*ca* 3000 BC) reveals the extraordinary number of sixty-four threads in the warp and forty-eight in the weft per square centimeter.

The horizontal loom, as well as the shuttle, were in general use among the people; the chief fibre woven was flax and occasionally wool. Wall pictures of shepherds with animal skins knotted over their shoulders are a rarity. Temples could be entered only in white clothing of vegetable fibres. A thinner thread than that of flax could be spun from the fibre of the Sudanese cotton tree. The transparent over-garments from Byssus enjoyed great popularity with both men and women and were later much sought after in the neighbouring countries to the north-east. In ancient Athens and Rome the ladies showed themselves off in transparent Byssus garments imported from Egypt, the charm of which was sung by the poets.

In the beginning male clothing, as has been mentioned, consisted of a short and comparatively narrow loincloth, which later reached to the mid-calf. In its longer form it was wide in front and this part was either laid in folds or starched so that it projected in a pyramidal shape. In earlier times the upper garment was sleeveless and knotted over the left shoulder; later it had short or even long sleeves. In the New Kingdom the transparent overgarments of Byssus cloth appeared with wide, sloped out, wing-shaped sleeves that only covered the shoulders.

Whereas men's dress remained relatively unchanged, a vast number of modifications may be observed in women's dress. The close fitting white dress was painted with a net of coloured beads. Naturally the wearer of such a robe could not sit down, but apparently the ladies of ancient Egypt were already glad to suffer to be beautiful.

The treasure of Tut-ankh-Amon contains several shirts painted with a blue pattern resembling nets of beads. The pleat appears in every possible shape, in narrow longitudinal folds running the whole length of the garment, in the shape of rays on shoulder wraps and in a few instances even as transverse folds on sleeves. The wealth of necklines is positively bewildering. The neckline of the straight dress with broad shoulder straps begins just above the breast. Wedge-shaped necklines ending in a truncated point alternate with décolletés in which the wedge begins at the shoulder and reaches almost to the belt, so that half the breast was visible. Other dresses are only held on one shoulder, leaving one breast uncovered except for a light veil. Trimmings, ribbons, belts and fringes add a touch of colour to the gleaming white. Sometimes the whole garment was tinged with colour that paled towards the hem of the skirt. During the Late period metal appliqués came into fashion; they were distributed at regular intervals in the same way as modern spangles, and were even used over the painted nets of beads. How the needles were made remains an open question. During the early dynasties they were still of copper, since bronze was not manufactured till later. The eye was not bored. It must have been pierced with a very fine tool which did not, however, cause any visible lateral expansion of the metal. What considerably harder material was used for this piercer? Copper a relatively soft metal, can be rendered harder by hammering, but scarcely to the necessary degree.

After the continual invasions of various foreign races during the Late period a nostalgic longing for the golden age of the Old Kingdom was felt, which was also mirrored in jewellery and dress. The resulting style is anachronistic, confused and totally lacking in unity. When, after Alexander the Great, the Ptolemies had themselves portrayed on temple walls in the traditional garb and posture of the pharaohs and dressed up in ancient Egyptian style for acts of state, this was hardly in keeping with the times. All images on coins, on the other hand, show the rulers as belonging in appearance, hairstyle and dress, so far as this is to be seen, including the crown, to the world of Greek civilization. On her coins, Cleopatra is always shown wearing her hair parted and held in a chignon low on the neck, and with a prominent aquiline nose. On the temple of Dendera, where she is to be seen as the pharaoh, her features have been frozen into the conventional mould demanded by tradition. The spread of the Isis cult outside Egypt brought about a fashion which was meant to look ancient Egyptian, but this soon vanished never to return.

The Toilet

Great importance was attached to cleanliness. In *La vie quotidienne en Egypte* P. Montet mentions a soaplike paste that lathered and dissolved fat. It probably contained ash and alumina. There is some justification for the belief that the Egyptians discovered something approaching soap through the use of natron in mummifying.

How did they keep their houses free from insects? The Ebers Papyrus in Leipzig gives us the answer: they washed the floors with a solution of salts of natron. As the climate demanded, the Egyptian washed several times a day and washed his hands and rinsed his mouth before and after every meal. Because of the heat, he also changed his clothes several times a day. If he was on a long journey, one of his retinue was charged with carrying the sack of clean clothes. This custom also applied to his journey into the Next World, as a *ushabti* figure in the Cairo Museum shows.

Shaving and cutting the hair was done by the barber. He visited the rich in their houses, if they did not maintain a personal barber. His poorer customers he attended to on a stool in the shade of a sycamore. He also had at his disposal a cure for baldness: an oil derived from the seeds of the box thorn. This plant, called in Arabic *helba*, is still employed for many purposes as a household remedy and in pharmaceutics. Prescriptions against body odour played a great role. Perfumes and essences were very popular with both women and men. Body hair was considered unhygienic; priests were allowed to enter the temple only after the removal of all hair. Toe and finger nails were kept short. In the Old Kingdom in particular men used to wear thin, shaved moustaches similar to those of today. In the New Kingdom the ends of the eyebrows and the outer corners of the eyes were extended with kohl, which was applied with a fine bronze pencil.

The double containers for various tinting preparations are particularly attractive. The simple but well-proportioned palette for cosmetics in six colours from the funerary treasure of Tut-ankh-Amon has become world famous. There are innumerable variants of the unguent jars of glazed and unglazed earthenware, or more rarely wood, coloured glass or ivory. When the container rests upon a human figure it becomes a work of art unparalleled in any other culture. Artistic inventiveness seems to have been particularly fertile in the working of coloured glass.

Woman Carrying Duck. The close-fitting dress with shoulder straps begins just below the breast. It is covered with a pattern of glazed faience beads. To render the movement of striding, an extremely skilful optical illusion has been created in the process of painting. The top and bottom row of beads run horizontally, while the middle rows follow the swelling of the thigh in a downward curve. (Tomb of Mektj-re, end of the Middle Kingdom, Cairo Museum.)

HARVESTING FLAX. Linen was the favourite dress material in ancient Egypt. A man and his wife are together pulling up the flax stems in bunches. (Tomb No. 1, Senedjem, 20 Dyn., Deir el-Medina.)

Loom. Women at a horizontal loom. A spindle may be seen on the left. Size of the figures 8–9 cm. Painted wooden model placed in tomb. (End of the Middle Kingdom, Cairo Museum.)

Weaver's Reed. The reed of a loom. The crosspieces are split lengths of hard cane, the wooden frame is covered with lacquered fabric. Standing, a reel with twisted flax. Beside it a ball of flax. (Date doubtful, Cairo Museum.)

Courtier Bowing. Over his hair is a cap with a neck protector. The half-length sleeves have horizontal folds. The front of the ceremonial loincloth is pleated lengthways, the pleats being rounded at the bottom. (Tomb No. 55, Ramose, 18 Dyn., Sheikh Abdel Gurna.)

Priest with Cleanshaven Head. Priest in the posture of prayer, wearing the robe that is put on over the head, with half-length sleeves and ceremonial apron in front. Priests had to be devoid of all hair. (Tomb No. 96, Senefer, 20 Dyn., Dier el-Medina.)

Garb of Man and Wife. The man's close-fitting over-garment with short sleeves ends above the knees. From the waist down he has a long, transparent loincloth. His wife is wearing the simple dress with shoulder straps. (Tomb No. 96, Senefer, 20 Dyn., Sheikh Abdel Gurna.)

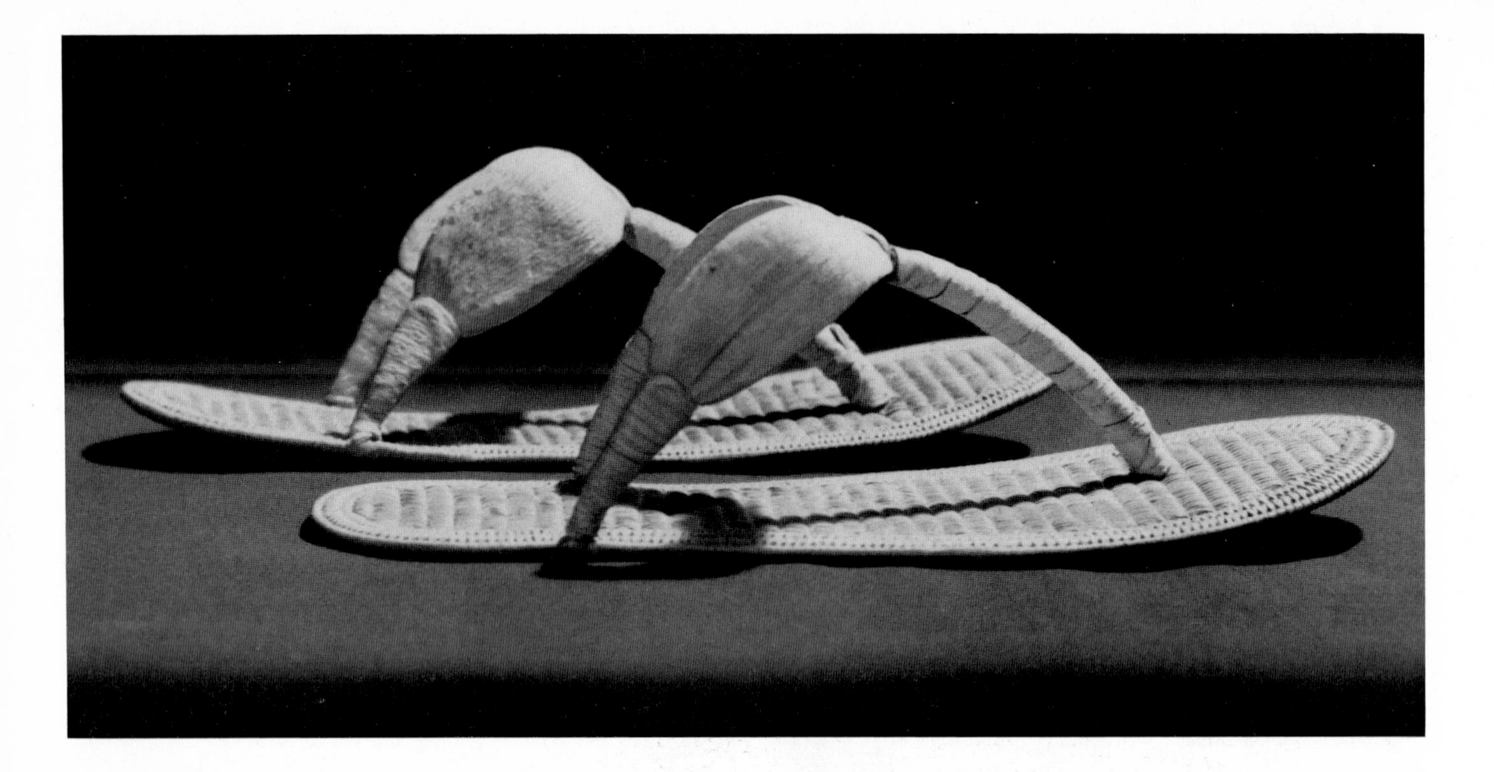

BAST SANDALS. The design combines perfect fitness for purpose with beauty of line. Archaeological evidence proves that they come from the tomb of Jujia and Tujia, the maternal grandparents of Akhenaton. (18 Dyn., Cairo Museum.)

RELIEF SHOWING SANDALS. Sandals for outdoor wear were of leather. The vertical side pieces are attached to the sole, not visible here, and hold the foot straps, which go round the heel. (Great Temple, detail from the 4th pylon, Karnak, 19 Dyn.)

Lady in Ceremonial Dress. The ceremonial wig frames a face which, in spite of being damaged, is still beautiful in its nobility and sovereign inner calmness. Only the eyes and eyebrows have been picked out in black. The exceptionally charming figure is in delightful contrast to the gravity of the face and head. The dress and the shoulder-wrap tied under the breast are of gauze-thin pleated lawn. (Crystalline limestone, 19–20 Dyn., Cairo Museum.)

FESTAL ROBE. Over the under-dress, which shows through, a cloaklike wrap whose fringe ends in little knots. The head ornament consists of a broad band tied at the back with petals attached to it. In the front a lotus flower. The cone on top of the head is thought to be wax impregnated with perfume. The hair falls freely over shoulders and back in thin plaits. The wife of Senedjem. (Tomb No. 1, 20 Dyn., Deir el-Medina.)

LAWN DRESS. Only times of the highest wordly triumph, such as the rule of Ramses II, could produce such a combination of sensuous, plastic life with artistic refinement. Over the long, pleated robe lies a wrap with a ribbon tied at the breast. The narrow girdle with its horizontal folds forms a counterpoint to the vertical pleats. Queen Nefertari, wife of Ramses II. (19 Dyn., Temple of Amon, Luxor.)

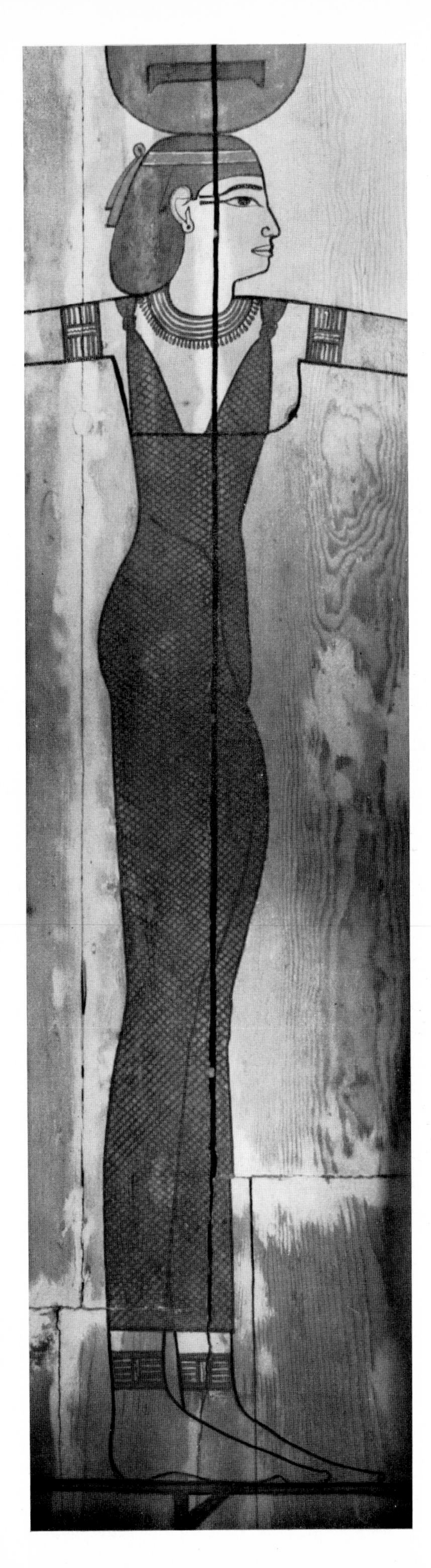

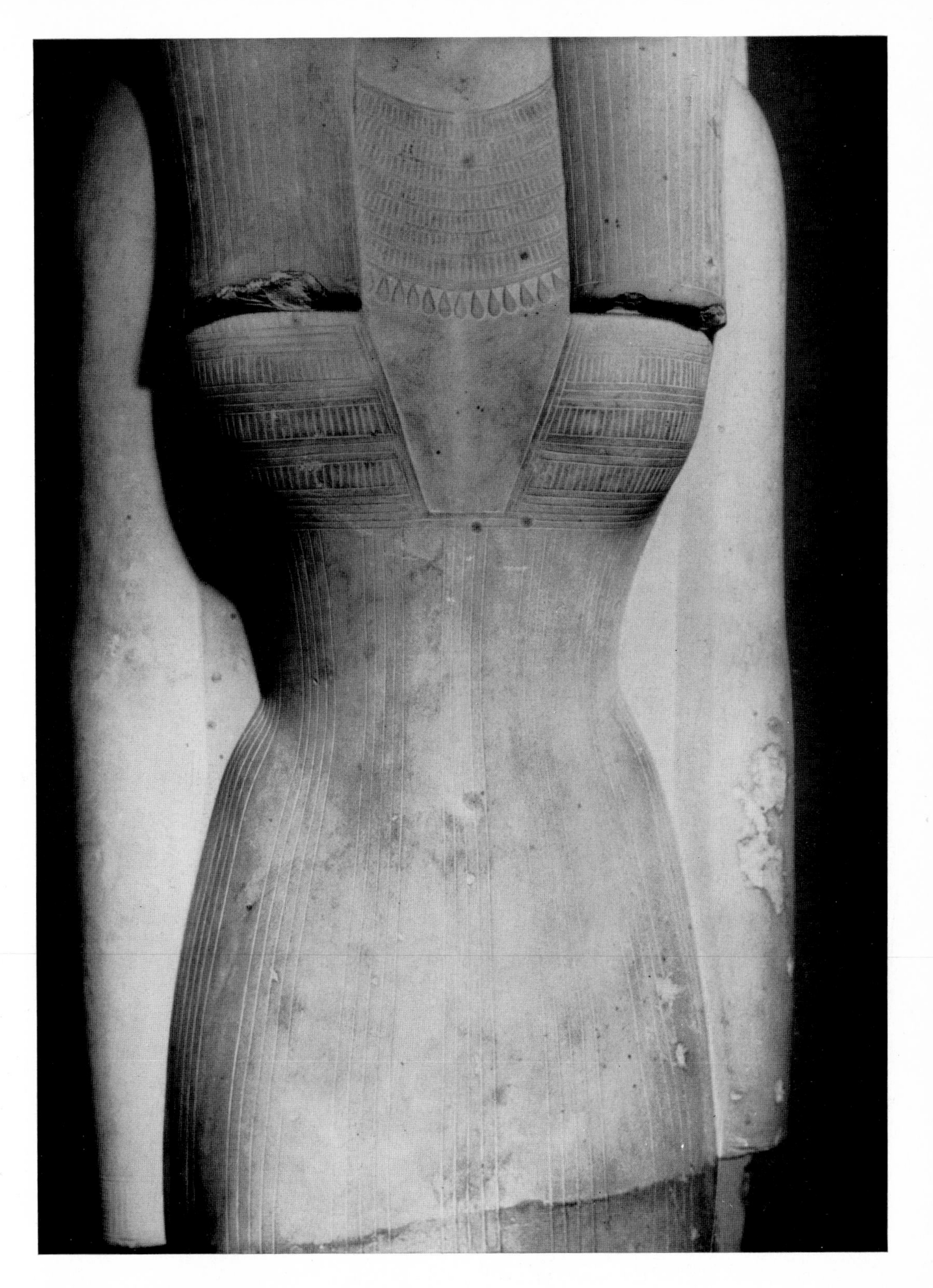

NET DRESS. A dark reddish-brown, close-fitting net dress with straps knotted on the shoulders in the style of the Late period. The hatched method of painting allows breasts, hips and legs to show through. In addition the ground tone of the body is darker towards the edges, producing a three-dimensional effect. Interior of a sarcophagus. The Queen of Heaven's arms stretch out protectively over the side walls. Cedarwood. (Beginning of the Late period, Cairo Museum.)

DRESS WITH A WEDGE-SHAPED DECOLLETE. The sleeveless dress has a deep, wedge-shaped décolleté. The delicate fabric is reinforced with fine transverse and vertical seams. In their groups of four, the vertical seams form a pattern. Judged by its style this masterpiece would appear to date from the Middle Kingdom, but it probably comes from the Late period. During this epoch, with its neo-classical tendencies, copies of earlier models were popular. Particularly brittle, compact limestone. (Late period, 19 Dyn., Cairo Museum.)

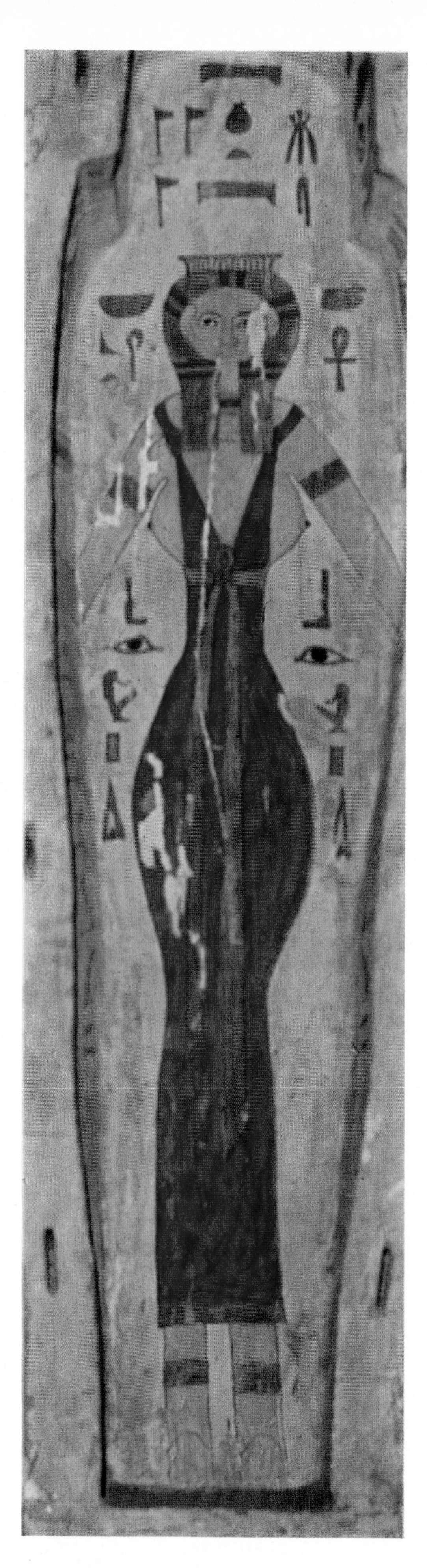

Dress with Deep Decollete. Close-fitting red dress with shoulder straps that leave the breasts free. The wasp-waist is displaced upwards by means of the bluish-green belt, which is directly under the bust. So much emphasis on the female attributes was only possible in the decadent era at the end of the Late period. The frontal position is rare in painting. Unlike the preceding picture of the net dress, the protective arms of the Queen of Heaven, Mut, point downwards. (Interior of a sarcophagus, end of the Late period, Cairo Museum.)

Unguent-pot Bearer. The shape of the unguent pot, which is determined purely by its practical purpose, and the finely profiled sculpture of the kneeling bearer combine through their mutually determined proportions to form a work of art. On the lower part of the side of the pot a leaping calf has been inlaid in ivory. Red-tinted wood. Natural size. (New Kingdom, Cairo Museum.)

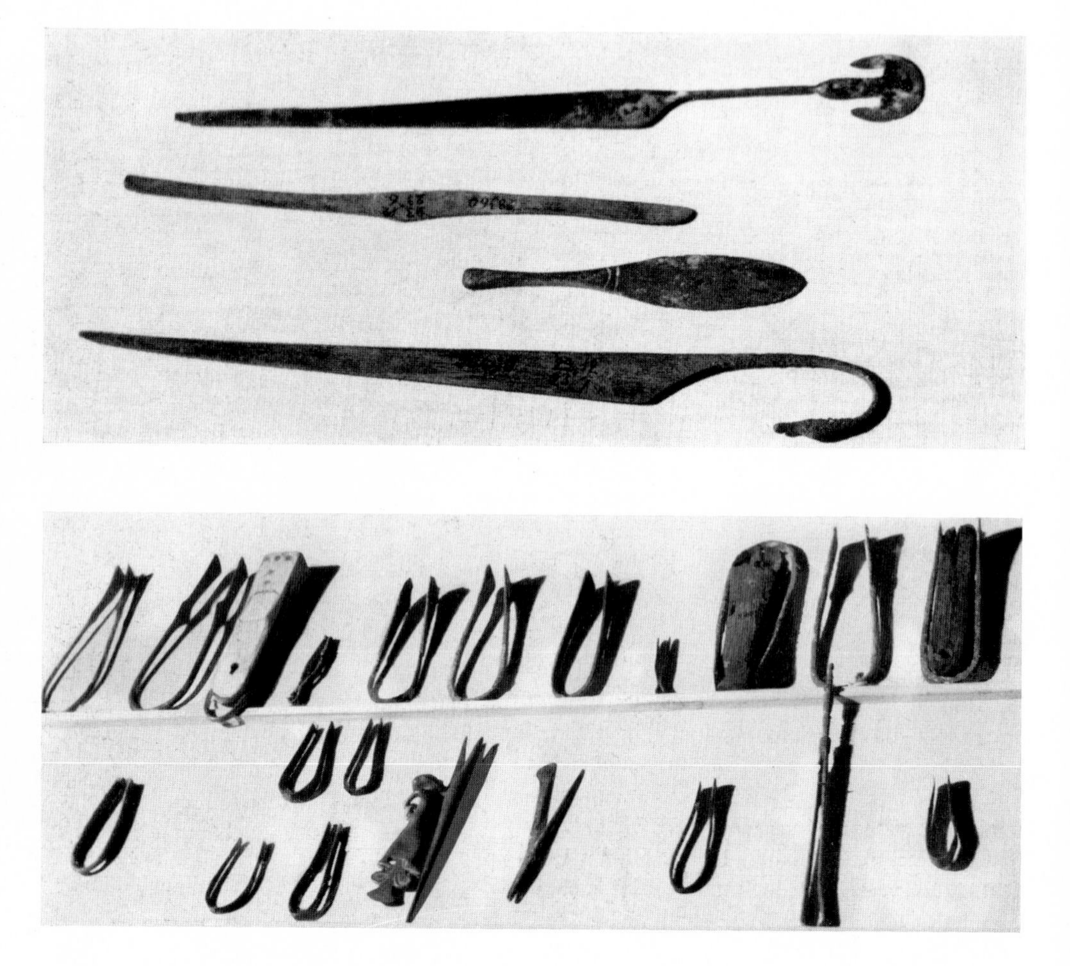

COMBS. Combs were made of wood or bone. This selection of wooden combs shows in the upper row: Combs with teeth on one side and protrusions on the back to give a better grip. In the centre: a fine comb with a long handle. Below: Double-sided combs with narrow and wide teeth. (Cairo Museum.)

RAZORS. Razors were in use at the very earliest period. Those illustrated here are from the New Kingdom. The second from top, in particular, is in keeping with our own idea of a razor in its long, narrow shape. (New Kingdom, Cairo.)

PINCERS AND SCISSORS. Bronze pincers were employed chiefly for plucking the eyebrows. Below centre: Two pairs of scissors. The pair with a human figure attached date from the New Kingdom. (Cairo Museum.)

HAIR CUTTING. Workers (recruits?) are having their hair cut. In the upper row they are sitting on folding-stools, in the lower on three-legged stools. On the ground in front of the barber a bowl. (Tomb No. 56, Userhat, 18 Dyn., Sheikh Abdel Gurna.)

LADIES AND A SERVING GIRL. Young serving girl straightening an earring. The only clothing worn by the graceful girl is a girdle made up of strings of small faience beads. The clothes of the ladies leave the left breast free, but it is lightly covered by a transparent wrap falling over the arm. The natural posture of the seated women is free from conscious coquetry but has the charm of instinctive vanity. (Tomb No. 57, Nakht, 17 Dyn., Sheikh Abdel Gurna.)

COSMETIC CONTAINER. Wooden cosmetic box in the shape of a duck. The wings form the lid and open at the sides. In the background: Container for eye kohl in the shape of a column of coloured glass paste; the bronze pencil projects from it. Right: Container of bluish-green pottery with two separate tubes for two kinds of kohl. (New Kingdom, Cairo Museum.)

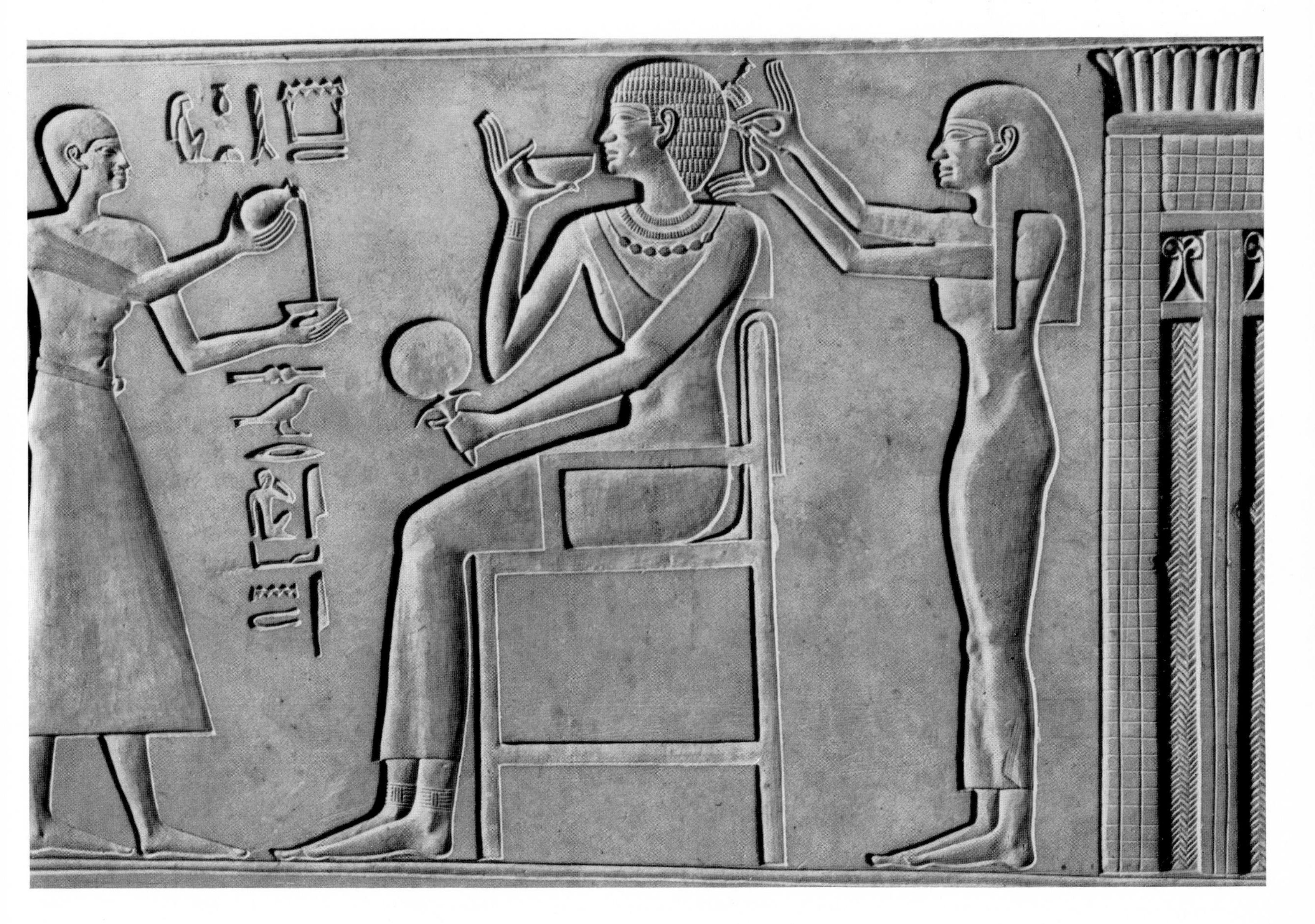

LADY AT HER TOILET. A lady is having her hair done. The last lock is just being curled. The hair-slide, looking like a pennon, has already been inserted. In her right hand the lady is holding a bowl of fresh milk, in her left the indispensable mirror. (Queen Kawit, 12 Dyn., Cairo Museum.)

Scent Bottles and Salve Jars. (three-quarter natural size). Glassblowing was not discovered till the beginning of our era. In Egypt, opaque glass was manufactured by a far more laborious process. Feather-glass, so-called on account of the feather-like pattern, was in the ancient world a valued collector's piece for which astonishingly high prices were paid. Egyptian glass bowls were carried in the triumphal procession of the Emperor Augustus. Rome later had to erect stringent tariff barriers to prevent the ruinous import of coloured glasses from Egypt. In the foreground a scent bottle with a glass top. (New Kingdom, Cairo Museum.)

The human need for jewellery may already be seen in its most primitive form among the hunters of prehistory, who demonstrated their successes in the chase by attaching feathers to their persons or hanging the claws and teeth of their prey round neck and limbs. Women, on the other hand, made necklaces and bracelets from shells and splinters of crystal, which were often coloured. If the prehistoric Egyptian shaped bones, ivory and semi-precious stones into generally irregular balls, cones and drops, or worked steatite beads, this was conscious manufacture. Even the use of gold is known to us from the Neolithic period. The Cairo Museum possesses a flint knife whose handle is coated with gold-leaf and bears representations of human beings and animals.

Jewellery and gold

The inhabitants of the Nile Valley were already wearing a great deal of jewellery at the beginning of the Dynastic era and the custom was maintained right down to the Late period. The manufacture of jewellery had acquired great importance by the time of the first dynasties and called for considerable skill on the part of the goldsmith. This assertion is justified by the few, but exceptionally beautiful pieces that have been preserved in spite of thousands of years of tomb robbing. The bracelets from the beginning of the First Dynasty come from Abydos, the site of the tomb of the pharaoh Djer or Zer, who is considered to be the third ruler of the united country. His name is a hieroglyph: the falcon of Horus on the façade of a palace. The jewellery was found on a separate mummified arm wrapped in linen bandages. There is no basis for the assumption that it belongs to the mummy of the king's wife, since anatomical examination failed to establish the arm bones as female. For the higher classes semi-precious stones such as amethyst, turquoise, lapis-lazuli, green feldspar and onyx were worked; the populace contented themselves with faience jewellery, in which the colours green, blue and white predominated. Occasionally we find small inlays of carnelian and rock-crystal in the shape of small beads or cut into rods. The skill of the artist-craftsmen responsible for the moulding, firing and glazing of rings, necklaces, bracelets and amulets is extraordinary, since they were in many cases working on a minute scale and magnifying glasses were as yet unknown. Furthermore, this kind of jewellery must have been comparatively cheap, since countless fragments have been found in the soil of the country. Rings and amulets of bronze date mostly from the New Kingdom and the Late Dynastic period. Apart from the magic character of certain inscriptions, amulets show a wealth of popular religious and mythological symbols. Above all, the eye of Horus, the pillar of Osiris and the knot of Isis, to name but three. Naturally, young married women wore the well-known fertility symbols, such as the amulet of Isis giving her breast to her son Horus.

The early discovery of glass and the peculiarity of the materials employed by the Egyptians led to the method of mixing pounded semi-precious stones with the fluid glass. These coloured glass pastes were then cut into the desired shapes after cooling.

Gold was very seldom used as jewellery by the secular castes. It was sacred to the deities and their temples and reserved for religious purposes. In the Old and Middle Kingdom the precious metal was worked exclusively in the temple precincts into bowls, goblets and statuettes, carefully catalogued and registered as the property of the deity. It could be worn publicly as jewellery by the pharaoh (as the son of god and his representative on earth) and his closest relatives, but the priests were permitted to wear it only on special occasions. Gold was also bestowed as a gift upon friendly kings and vassal princes.

It was the taste for display that developed at the end of the New Kingdom which brought about the relaxation of these strict rules. In particular, women began to wear gold jewellery. When necessary, gold was hardened by the admixture of copper; the fire-gilding of non-precious metals was also known. Repeated smelting gave Egyptian gold a purity that has not been surpassed by modern methods. Mine-gold was obtained from the mountain ranges of Wawuat and from Wadi Hammamat, river-gold from Kush in Upper Nubia. The Turin Museum possesses a papyrus showing the coloured plan of a gold mine with the names of all the galleries.

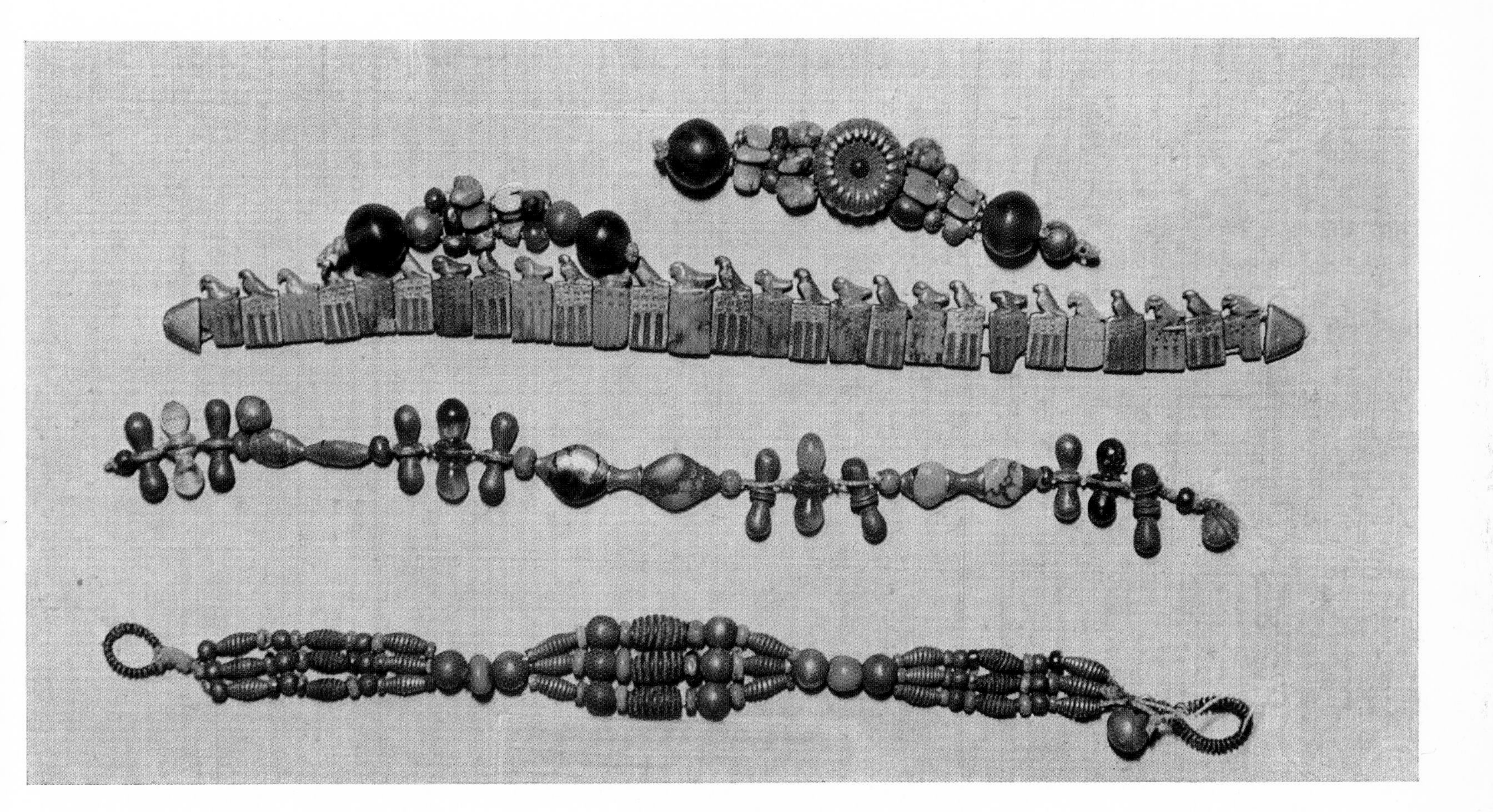

FOUR BRACELETS. These bracelets are the only pieces of jewellery in existence that can be proved to date from the First Dynasty. Apart from gold, amethyst, purple lazuli and turquoise were employed. Three of the bracelets show decorative patterns, the second from the top a figurative drawing: a row of hawks of Horus perched on the façade of a palace. Note that the turquoise hawks are perched over six window apertures, those of gold over twelve. The royal seal of the First Dynasty was (with slight modifications) the hawk of Horus. (Tomb of the pharaoh Djser, from Abydos, 1 Dyn., Cairo Museum.)

Decorative Collar and Armband. The Queen of Heaven, Hathor, wearing a broad blue, white and red collar. Armbands of this type consist of metal fillets divided up into cells and inlaid with cut pieces of coloured glass paste like cloisonné. (Tomb of Horemhab, 17 Dyn., Valley of the Kings, West Thebes.)

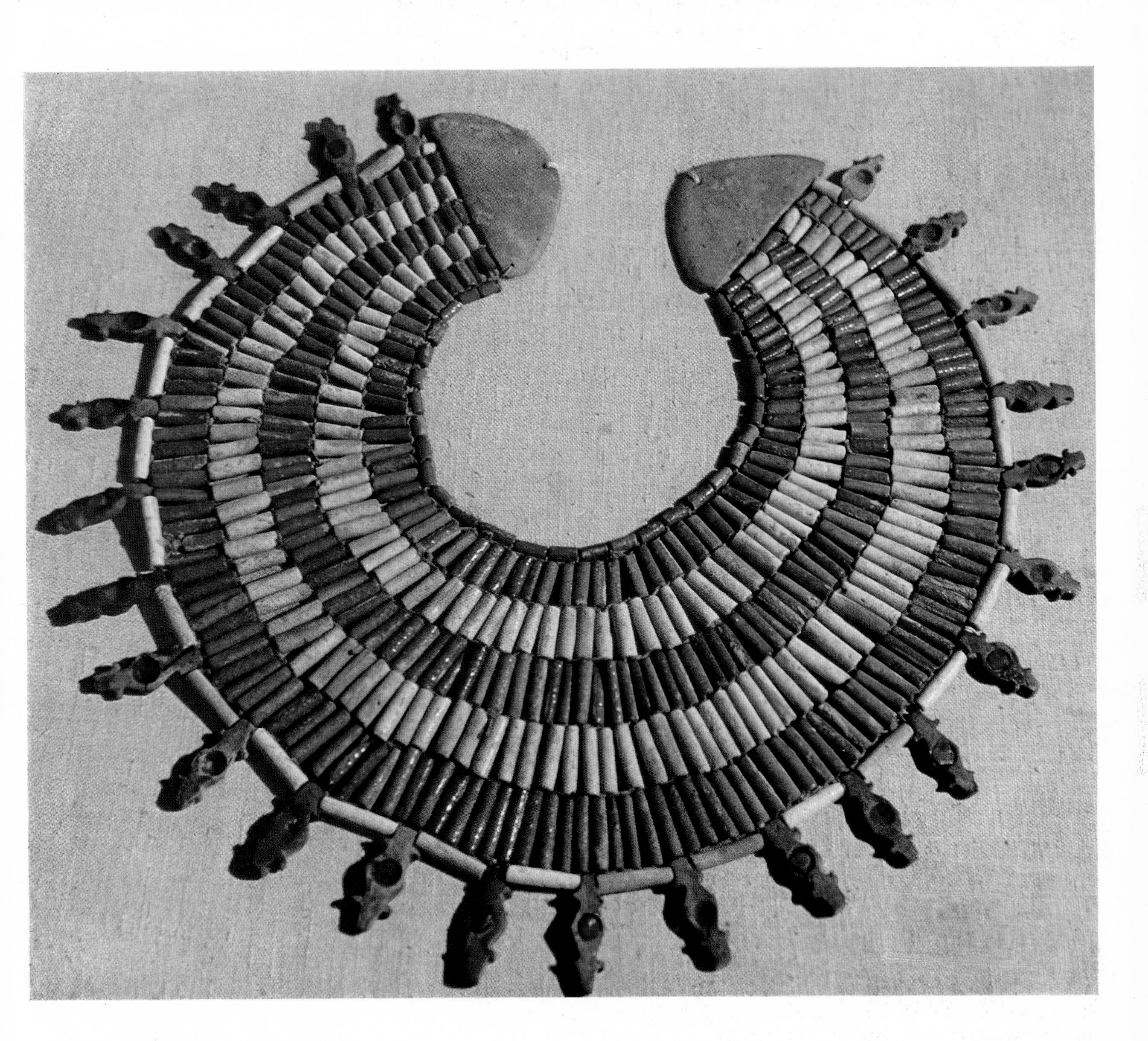

COLLAR OF FAIENCE BEADS. The beads are tubular in shape and glazed. Some of the projecting beads still contain in their centre imitation carnelians, produced by laying red earth colour in the hollows and inlaying rounded pieces of crystal on top of it. (Funerary treasure of Tut-ankh-Amon, 18 Dyn., Cairo Museum.)

FRIEZE OF GOLDSMITHS. Upper row *from left to right:* Weighing and registering the gold bars to be worked.—Melting the gold in a crucible resembling an inverted horn. The two crucibles shown here share one lid. The fire is kept hot by blowing vigorously through tubes. The air accumulates in the swelling in the lower end of the tube and streams out under strong pressure through the narrow opening.—A hole is made with a spike in the pointed end of the crucible and the melted gold is poured into moulds.—Lower row *from right to left:* Chasing the ornament. The graver may be seen in the hand of the dwarf.—Showing off a finished collar. (Tomb of Mereruka, 5 Dyn., Sakkara.)

GIRLS WITH COLLARS. Two girls wearing earrings, shoulder-wide collars and broad headbands with petals attached. On their heads a cone of myrrh. One of the girls is holding up a wide collar admiringly. The softness of the fingers and the loose, unplaited hair show the influence of Amarna. (Tomb of Djeser-Kara-Senneb, 18 Dyn., Sheikh Abdel Gurna.)

TWO NECKLACES. Outer necklace: Opaque glass beads, ceramic rings and in the upper part light carnelian. Below very dark carnelian. Inner necklace: Small yellow ceramic rings, eye of Horus increasing in size, greenish colour. In the middle: Amulets. Above, figure of a dwarf; below, two baboons, cat seen in profile, amulet bearing written characters, and an amulet bearing a human figure. (Middle Kingdom, Cairo Museum.)

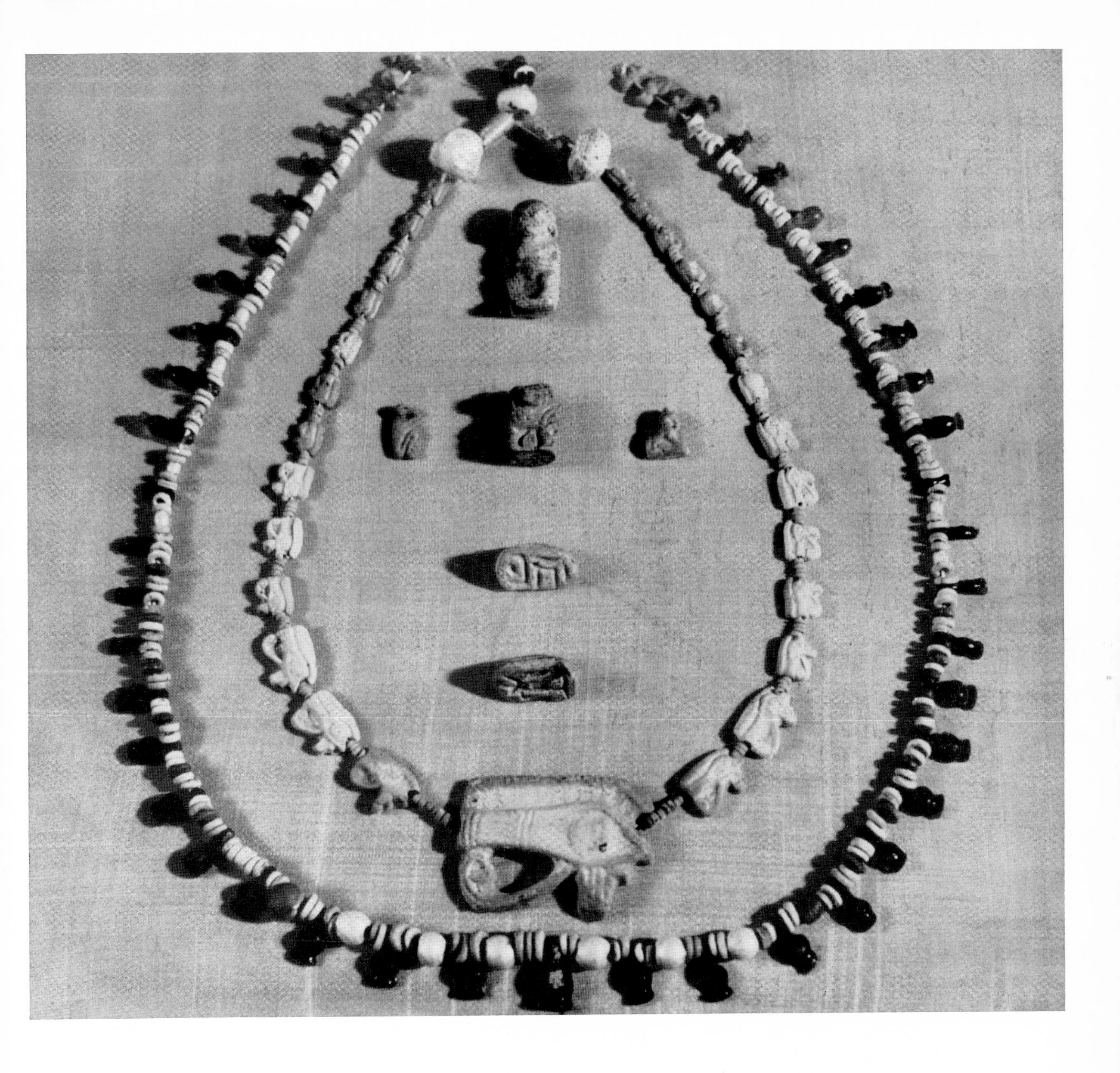

FINGER RINGS. *From left to right*, upper row: Carnelian ring; two bronze rings, one bearing an inscription, the other a marguerite. Lower row: sideways on, a lotus blossom and a uraeus crowned with the sun disc. Lotus blossom and a uraeus. Two hawks of Horus crowned by a sun disc. Glazed earthenware. (New Kingdom and Late period, Cairo Museum.)

HAIR RINGS. Carnelian rings of various sizes. The strands of hair were pulled in through the slit at the side and tied. (Middle Kingdom, Cairo Museum.)

The family

Historical misunderstandings have a curiously tenacious life, particularly when they have been, so to speak, legitimized by references to classical authors. In the following paragraphs we shall discuss the concept of sibling marriage. "Ancient Egypt" is an inescapable collective term covering a span of time of at least three thousand years. Inevitably, it embraces apparent historical discrepancies and contradictions. In spite of the empire's great continuity Egypt cannot be looked upon as a closed, unchanging entity. Over a period of several thousand years such incidents as reversion to earlier trends, foreign domination, internal revolutions and religious conflicts form part of a nation's natural course of development.

If, therefore, authors of classical antiquity such as Herodotus, Diodorus and Pliny manifestly contradict one another as to certain details of their undoubtedly credible accounts, each of them nevertheless made his report in good faith. First of all, we must bear in mind the difference between the dates at which the various accounts were written, then the natural differences between the northern and southern section of the country, and finally the possibility of misleading interpretations of certain terms in the process of translating from ancient Egyptian into Greek or Latin.

In mythology, the divine brother and sister Osiris and Isis with their son Horus represented the epitome of the family as early as the Old Kingdom. Osiris and Isis were sent to earth by the Supreme God to raise men from their primeval condition and announce to them God's omnipotence and goodness. Divine beings could only unite with their peers. After Osiris's death, Isis mourned her brother and husband. These mourning laments are among the most beautiful things in ancient Egyptian literature and as such were inherited and passed on from generation to generation. On the basis of this tradition we must understand that the words "brother" and "sister" are to be equated with beloved. In the love songs of the New Kingdom the poet longs for his good, beautiful, desirable "sister". In Egypt the word sister means the person to be loved, if not already the lover. Thus the wife addresses her husband, away on military service, as "distant brother". This custom and the literal translation into Greek and Latin may have given rise in antiquity to a belief in the general practice of sibling marriage among the ancient Egyptians. Members of the royal family, in particular the pharaoh, entered into marriage with blood relations. Among high dignitaries, priests who were commoners, and the common people, this would have been unthinkable, since it would in a sense have raised them to the status of gods. Monogamy was the rule throughout the country, but if his first wife remained childless the husband was permitted to keep additional wives whose offspring were recognized as legitimate children. Hence we can understand how it came about that Herodotus wrote of monogamy and Diodorus of polygamy.

All artistic representations show the husband beside one wife, and the papyri also always refer to one wife. She was in unquestioned command of the house and the education of the children. The son was not allowed to be punished by his father; this was the function of a male relative of his mother. The father introduced his son to his craft when he became a youth. The advice left by a father to his grown-up son runs: "Multiply the bread that you give to your mother, carry her as she carried you." The property and inheritance of the wife remained at her exclusive disposal even in marriage; the daughter inherited from her mother. A woman could not hold any public office, but she frequently engaged in commerce with great success. For ladies of the higher classes the activity of priestess seems to have been a kind of honorary function. Several women have gone down in history as queens in their own right.

We know little about the conclusion of a marriage as a spiritual ceremony or a worldly contract, but a great deal about the punishments for adultery. Men were scourged and women publicly marked by having their noses cut off. The image of Isis seated and giving her breast to Horus was to be seen on every domestic altar. This symbol of motherhood was worn by women and girls as an amulet, of glazed faience, carved in wood or bone or mass-produced in hundreds of thousands in moulded bronze. The cult of Isis conquered parts of Greece and spread via Rome and Treves as far as Britain.

THE ANHOUR-KAW FAMILY. Anhour-Kaw and his wife Wabet, surrounded by their sons and daughters. The girls are holding quails in their hands. The father is doing his daughter's hair. On the right of the picture, a basket of figs seen from above. (Tomb No. 359, Anhour-Kaw, 19 Dyn., Deir el-Medina.)

Isis with Horus. Isis nursing her son Horus became at a very early period a symbol of motherhood among the people. At all periods of the Egyptian Empire, Isis amulets protected mothers-to-be. (Statue from a domestic altar, Late period, Cairo Museum.)

Woman in Labour. Two midwives are helping a woman in labour. On the left: A second pregnant woman. Cracks have resulted in parts of the stone shifting sideways, spoiling the picture as a whole. (From the mastaba of Ankh-ma-hor, Sakkara, beginning of the 6 Dyn.)

MILKING. The cow is shedding a tear because the milker is taking away the milk intended for her calf. After severe internal disturbances, the country recovered its unity in the Middle Kingdom. In art too there was a return to the example of the early dynasties, to the "Golden Age." Although the whole composition is appealing, it does not quite measure up to its model: the man's foot is not divided up into its component parts, the calf's hoofs seem to be floating in the air. (Sarcophagus of Queen Kawit, 11 Dyn., Cairo Museum.)

WORKING MOTHER. The woman is carrying her child in the cloth slung round her shoulder. The last fruit from the tree that has now been plucked bare is being placed in the bowl. (Tomb No. 52, Nakht, 18 Dyn, Sheikh Abdel Gurna.)

THREE DOLLS. sawn from a flat piece of wood and painted; head and arms are rudimentary. The hair on the left is made up of a series of unfired clay beads. That on the right is loosely plaited flax. (Date uncertain, Cairo Museum.)

THE KISS. The kiss as a chaste caress consisted in a tender rubbing together of noses. The resulting interchange of breath was symbolically related to the idea of the breath of life. Depictions are known of the Godhead conveying his breath to the pharaoh. The lip kiss, on the other hand, is found in erotic pictures, especially those of the Late period. An unfinished statue of the pharaoh Akhenaton (with crown) kissing a child. A rare portrayal of a kiss in sculpture, only possible during the "verist" period of Egyptian art. (From Tel el-Amarna, 18 Dyn., Cairo Museum.)

Children's Gymnastic and Dance Games. *From left to right*, top row: A boy balancing on his hands and feet on a comrade's shoulders. A tug-of-war without a rope; the feet pushing against each other in the centre indicate the boundary over which the opponent is to be pulled. Running game.—Middle row: A group of boys, each holding a feather; in the centre their leader with a handstaff. The boy squatting on the ground has to guess who hit him.—Bottom row: Girls have formed themselves into a living roundabout. The hieroglyphs above describe the game as "pressing grapes." A Hathor dance-game in which mirrors and wooden clappers in the shape of a hand are alternately crossed over each other. (Tomb of Mereruka, 5 Dyn., Sakkara.)

Children fighting and helping each other. Above: Two small girls pulling each other's hair. Below: One girl is pulling a thorn out of the other's foot. To be noted in each case is the "pure" profile view in our sense of the expression. (Tomb No. 69, Mena, 18 Dyn., Sheikh Abdel Gurna.)

Boy under a Date Palm. A boy is knocking down dates with stones. The lively movement of the boy as he bends back to throw is based upon the observation

of nature and has nothing further to do with traditional stereotypes for portraying the human figure. Probably a practise slab by apprentice sculptors. (End of the New Kingdom, Cairo Museum.)

GIRLS PLAYING. The girl on the left is snapping her fingers to beat out a time to which the other girl is hopping on one foot. A game or a dance? The long plaits end in woollen tassels. (Tomb of Mereruka, Sakkara, 5 Dyn.)

GIRLS WITH DUCKLING. The characteristic features of a living model and the obstinacy of an unconventional painter are expressed in this charming profile. The influence of the lifelike Amarna style is evident both in the plaits of hair blowing in the wind and in the ruffled down of the duckling. (Tomb No. 52, Mena, 18 Dyn., Sheikh Abdel Gurna.)

GIRL IN THE POSTURE OF PRAYER. Between the pillar-like legs of her father, the child is imitating the adults' attitude of worship. As is evident from the line of the garment running through the girl's thighs, the child was added later, probably at her father's request. (Tomb No. 345, Pashedu, 20 Dyn., Deir el-Medina.)

UNDER THE PROTECTION OF THE FATHER OF THE FAMILY. Two female figures are crouching beside the legs of the father of the family. The women's smile expresses joy at the consciousness of being under sure protection. There is particular tenderness in the hands which, instead of clasping, merely rest lightly on the legs. (Statue of Kawi, Sakkara, 6 Dyn., Cairo Museum.)

HUSBAND AND WIFE. In his tomb, Governor Ramose has had himself portrayed with his illustrious guests at a banquet. The reliefs are regarded as models of the noblest refinement combined with austere forms. The spatial distance between May and his wife Werel is overcome by her arm that passes behind her husband's back and holds his shoulder. (Tomb No 55, Ramose, 18 Dyn., Sheikh Abdel Gurna.)

MOTHER AND SON. This statue is exceptional in that it does not present the usual double portrait of a husband and wife, but of a mother and son. The family likeness is unmistakable in the cut of the eyes, the protruding cheekbones, the straight nose and strongly marked mouths. (Tuthmosis IV and Queen Teo, 18 Dyn., Cairo Museum.)

MOURNING WOMEN. From right to left: The woman bending forward is comforting the woman in mourning. The woman sitting behind is putting her arm round her. Standing: Two women with raised hands and arms round each other's waist. Extreme left: A crouching woman with raised arm. The picture is one of communal mourning. (From the mastaba of Ankh-ma-hor, Sakkara, beginning of the 6 Dyn.)

THREE STOOLS. Above: A stool with inserted legs and elongated seat. Below left: A child's stool. Right: A four-legged stool. Seat and legs are carved from the same block; the seat is hollowed out. (Middle and New Kingdom, Cairo Museum.)

SIMPLE CHAIR WITH FOOT REST. Chair with a high back curved at the top. The seat is woven from twisted reed leaves. The wood of both chair and foot rest is joined with pegs and grooves. (End of the New Kingdom—beginning of the Late period, Cairo Museum.)

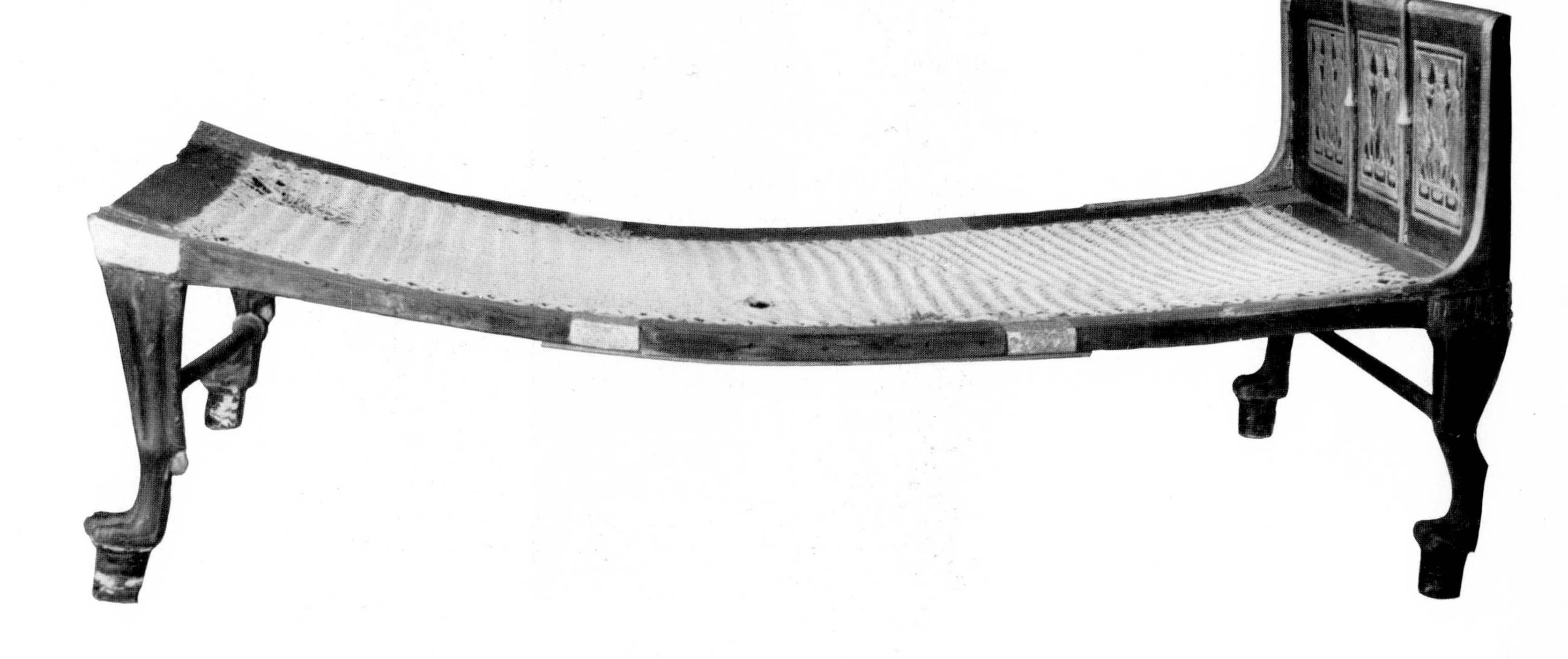

PORTRAYAL OF A BED. The poles in the foreground support the canopy. The bed rests on high lion's legs. Two servants are smoothing the sheet on the mattress. Under the bed as we see them, but actually conceived of as in front of it, a servant with two bags of linen not to be confused with pillows. (Tomb of Mehu, Sakkara, 5 Dyn.)

BED. Made of dark ebony with gilded fittings. The mattress is woven of fine flax cord. (New Kingdom, Cairo Museum.)

SENNEB AND HIS FAMILY. The name "Senneb" means "health" and thus counterbalances Sennebs' misshapen body. He held the post of administrator of the king's wardrobe. The children standing under their father form a sculptural counterpart to the legs of the mother and counteract the imbalance between the bodies of the two parents. The carefully protective pose of the wife expresses a joyful and conscious demonstration of her inseparability from her husband. (From Gizeh, 5 Dyn., Cairo Museum.)

Music and dancing

Music is one of mankind's earliest means of expression. We find the flute as the oldest wind instrument among all nomadic and pastoral peoples. Its development is shown in the increasing length of the pipe and the corresponding number of finger holes; it becomes the double flute and finally the multiple instrument, the so-called Pan pipes.

In the very earliest times the upper end of the pipe was not placed in the mouth, but in the nostrils. The Ice-Age cave of Les Trois Frères in southern France contains a wall-painting of a man dressed up as an animal trying to lure fleeing game by playing a nose-flute. At Oxford there is an archaic palette from Upper Egypt portraying beasts of prey and gazelles peacefully playing. In the lower

left-hand section a man is playing a nose-flute. Not until the Dynastic era was the flute blown with the mouth, and even later the blowing hole was placed at the side of the flute; then the upper end was closed.

The astonishing thing about the musical instruments of Egypt is that they occur in great variety and almost at the end-stage of their development as early as the Old Kingdom. The various types of percussion instrument were common, from the small hand-drum via the tambourine to the double-sided drum. The drums were beaten not with sticks, but with the fingers and the palms of the hands. Castanet-like wooden clappers hollowed out lengthways were also used. The Egyptians were familiar with many types of wind instrument, including many varieties of flute, culminating in the golden fanfares of Tut-ankh-Amon.

Stringed instruments were played without bows and plucked by hand. The earliest is probably the one-stringed mandola with an elongated oval sound-body and a resonance board consisting partly of skin and partly of a thin sheet of wood, with a sound-hole cut in it. The fret-board is long and the instrument is played with a wooden plectrum. Unlike the Greek lyre, the hand-harp in ancient Egypt was held horizontally and had seven strings. It was made in various sizes; the neck was curved well out to allow the hand great freedom of movement. The harp with eleven to thirteen strings, which stood on the ground, also existed in various forms. According to its size, the harpist stood or sat while playing.

A hand-rattle of metal, called by the Greeks *systrum* and adopted by them from the Egyptians, was reserved for religious purposes. It consisted of small metal discs loosely attached to several vertical rods that produced a tinkling sound when shaken. The *systrum* is still employed in almost unchanged shape in the Ethiopian Church. It was introduced into that country by Coptic monks spreading the Gospel.

Although the best known pictures from the New Kingdom almost without exception show blind harpists, while others portray lightly clad or naked dancing-girls playing musical instruments, we must not suppose that musicians formed a class which, apart from entertainment, had to provide base enjoyments. This may have occurred. But we also know tomb statuettes from the time of the pyramids bearing the proud inscription stating that the individual depicted had been a musician in the house of the prince or statesman so-and-so. In this, as in later epochs, sighted harpists are represented who, as minstrels, composed their own songs, some of them of the highest merit, as may be judged from the famous *Song of the Harper*.

Unfortunately musical notation was unknown. Attempts to deduce a scale from the finger positions seen in wall paintings and to establish a hypothetical notation on the basis of the arm and hand positions of the singers, are interesting but inconclusive. The water-organ invented in Alexandria by Ktesibius (3rd century BC) belongs to the Ptolemaic period and hence must be ascribed to the Greek genius, even though it took place on Egyptian soil.

Dancing

If finds made up to now tell us little about music, reliefs and wall paintings afford far more information about dancing.

For a start it must be stated as a basic fact that for the two sexes to dance together was unknown. If men or youths are shown dancing they are always single dancers surrounded by male spectators. Their heads are thrown back, their arms are not performing any fixed movements but generally hanging slackly by the side. Sometimes they are holding in their hands the castanet-like clappers already mentioned. The legs are stretched or slightly bent at the knee, the toes pointed downwards and always off the ground. It is a striking fact that the dancers (or would it be more accurate to call them jumpers?) display Negroid characteristics in both face and body. Occasionally the bystanders are depicted as clapping their hands. Accompaniment by musical instruments is totally absent. Hence what we are looking at is an athletic sport in which the performer went faster and faster to the accompaniment of rhythmic handclaps, rather than a dance.

The situation is different with regard to women. Two types of dancing can be distinguished: ritual and profane. The former took place at the head of festal processions and did not exclude such acrobatic dance figures as somersaults. The performance took place in the open air and hence was not temple dancing. In this kind of dancing the music was performed by priests, who followed directly behind the dancers. In the Old Kingdom, quite apart from the more austere style, the steps are more restrained, even though acrobatic postures also occur. At the time of the New Kingdom the row of dancers side by side was broken up and replaced by intersecting, more vigorously mobile groups. By and large the dances are manifestly made up of predetermined, repeated figures laid down by tradition. Dances in lines or groups were accompanied by musicians and almost always we see women clapping out the rhythm who are clearly distinguished by posture and dress from the dancers. They suggest at least supervisors, if not dancing teachers.

HARPIST (natural size). The harp and the body of the harpist are fused into a natural unity. The face with the tranquil smile is a fine expression of meditative joy in music-making. The Amarna style in its fully developed form may be seen in the full, soft lower part of the body, the folds over the stomach, the elongated neck and the sensitive face. (Limestone statuette with traces of colour, 18 Dyn., Cairo Museum.)

DOUBLE FLUTE AND MANDOLA. The female musician on the left is playing an unattached double flute. On the right a naked dancing girl is plucking a mandola. (Detail of a wall painting, Tomb No. 52, Nakht, 18 Dyn., Sheikh Abdel Gurna.)

LYRE. A lyre played in a horizontal position with outcurved stays to permit free movement of the hand. A rare feature in Egyptian art is the depiction of the palm of the hand with all the fingers in natural proportion to one another.

LARGE HARP. A female harpist standing with a large harp. In pictures large harps are generally shown with eleven, less frequently with fourteen strings. (Both pictures on this page: Tomb No. 38, Djeser-Kara-Senneb, 18 Dyn., Sheikh Abdel Gurna.)

Dancing Girls. The young dancing girls are wearing skirts above the knee tied with bows at the back; over the naked upper body crossing ribbons. Two dancing teachers are clapping out the rhythm for the measured step. (All three pictures: Tomb of Net-Heft-Ka, Sakkara, 5 Dyn., Cairo Museum.)

Singer and Flute-Player. The singer, recognizable by his parted lips, is giving the flute-player the time with his right hand. The left is placed to his ear in order to keep a better check on his own voice with the aid of head resonance. The twist of the flute-player's head is particularly intense as he literally reads off the sequence of notes from the singer's mouth.

Singer and Harpist. The way in which their two bodies are bent slightly towards each other illustrates the contact between the two musicians. Here again, it is obviously the singer who is setting the time.

Cymbals. Cymbals were fitted over the fingers with short leather slings and struck together. Their note was determined by the thickness of the disc, its diameter, the thickening round the edge and the height of the central curvature. They are probably a foreign import into the range of Egyptian musical instruments. (Late period, Cairo Museum.)

Mandola Players. The sound-board of the mandola consists of a stretched skin. The long, subdivided fret-board has only one string, which is struck with a wooden plectrum attached to the instrument with a string. The fact that they are playing in unison is shown by the identical positions of the hands. This impression is intensified by the arrangement of the musicians one behind the other. (New Kingdom, Great Temple, Karnak.)

DANCING GIRLS WITH TAMBOURINES. The dancing women are wearing transparent, cloak-like wraps. The middle figure is in the basic position, while the two others are performing right and left turns. The muscular thighs point to professional dancers. The movements of the dance are stressed by vertical wavy lines. Bottom right: two naked girls with castanet-like clappers. (Tomb of Khai, Sakkara, 18 Dyn., Cairo Museum.)

DANCING. The girls lean far back as they dance in unison to the rhythmic handclapping of the standing women. Their hair is tied in long strands ending in pompons. A neck-scarf hangs from the shoulders of their otherwise naked upper bodies. (Tomb of Mehru, Sakkara, 5–6 Dyn.)

Writing and scribes

"Hieroglyph" is a Greek word that has found its way into our vocabulary. It is made up of *hieros* = sacred and *glyphein* = to carve or write, and hence means literally "sacred writing." Since the Greeks, when they came to Egypt, saw these signs chiefly on temple walls, tomb stelae etc., they concluded that they must have a religious, sacred character. The ancient Egyptian script arose primarily out of representations of an object, a being or a process. From the single, separate pictorial sign (the true hieroglyph) the script passed by way of the simplified pictorial sign to the hieratic script, which was employed in official transactions and retained its religious character. To the majority of the literate population—and there were not many of them—it remained difficult to decipher. Popular speech was written down in the demotic cursive script. When writing fast, several pictorial signs would be run together, thus producing a new conceptual sign in which, however, the original elements are no longer recognizable. As a result it became necessary at the time of the Greek-speaking Ptolemies to publish an official memorandum like the Rosetta Stone in three scripts, namely hieroglyphic, demotic and Greek. By comparing the hieroglyphic text with the Greek, Champollion was able in 1822 to decipher the ancient Egyptian script. The hieroglyphs include a great many sound-symbols without, however, ever having constituted a complete alphabet. It was by taking the Egyptian written characters and modifying them that the Phoenicians formed the first complete alphabet used in the Mediterranean zone. Most European letters are derived from it.

Papyrus is another Greek word that lives on as "paper". The Greeks used it to describe a material hitherto unknown to them which the Egyptians employed for writing. It was made from the stem of the papyrus plant. Compared with the wax tablets in use in contemporary Europe, its advantages —greater durability and lower weight—were too evident for it not to come into universal use. Writing was done with reed pens and every writing set contained a red and a black writing-paste that was turned into ink ready for writing by the admixture of water. Writing was done in black; red was used to emphasize important words, for borders and for underlining.

The script requires the scribe. In view of the varieties of Egyptian scripts, namely hieroglyphic, hieratic and demotic, we may assume that not every scribe had mastered all three.

The ever-expanding profession of scribe developed into a new class, the class of state officials. After the rulers and priests, they formed the most important caste in the country. We must not picture the scribe as a subordinate pen-pusher, although there were such men among them. The scribe was called upon to think for himself and where necessary to enforce respect for his orders. Thus scribes are known who filled the posts of leaders of expeditions, architects and even judges. The objective designation of a profession came to be used as an honoured title. Akhthoes advises his son: "Learn to write, for this will be of greater advantage to you than all the other trades I have enumerated to you. One day at school is useful to you, and the work done there will endure for an eternity, like mountains."

SCRIBE. The method of drawing the eye may be particularly clearly seen in this statue of an unknown scribe. The encircling lines are of copper, the eyeball of bone, the pupil of cut crystal with a background of ebony and in the centre a copper pin. Through their knowledge and ability scribes occupied an exalted position in the State. They constituted the prototype of the civil servant. (From Sakkara, 4 Dyn., Cairo Museum.)

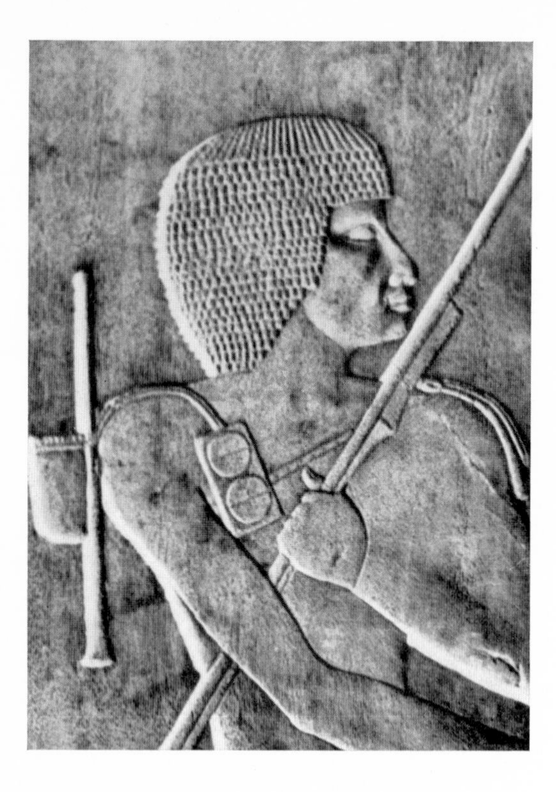

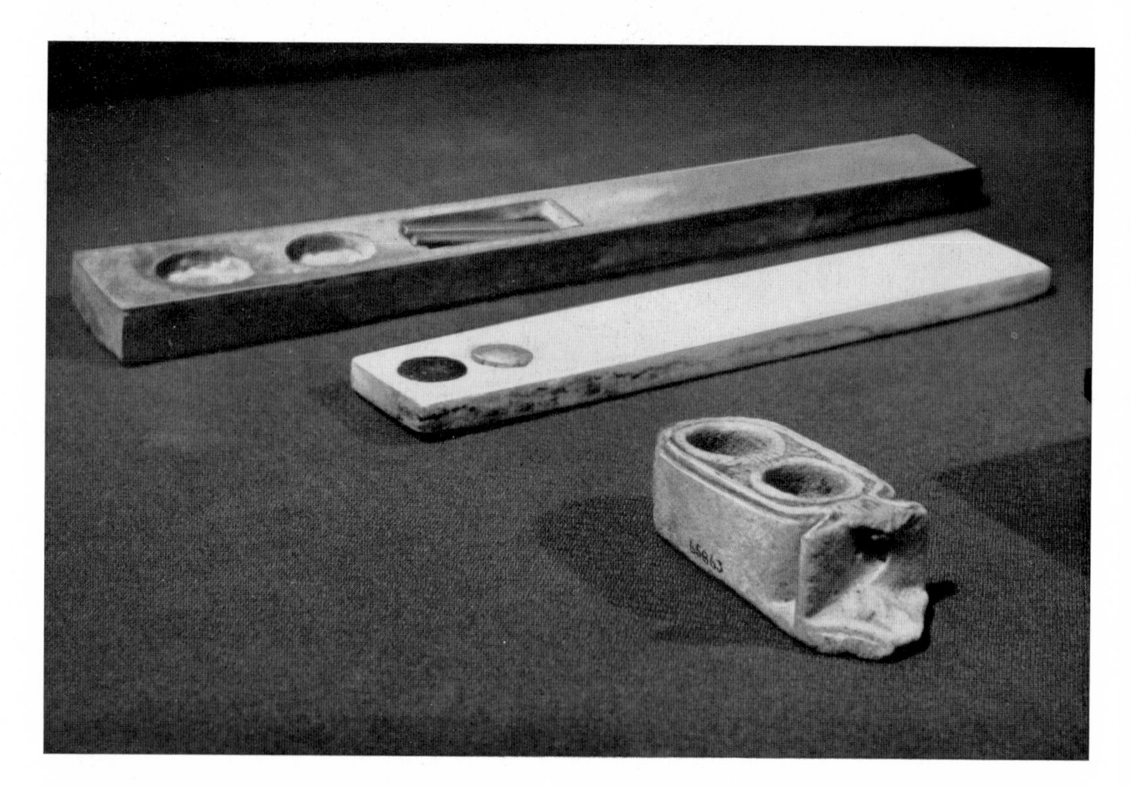

WRITING PALETTE (section). The early writting palette consisted of a small board with holes for the red and black coloured paste. Attached to it was the leather pouch for water with which to moisten the pastes. The mouth of this pouch could be closed by drawing tight a cord. The ideogram for writing is always the short palette, although writing implements underwent important changes. (Hesire, Sakkara, 4 Dyn., Cairo Museum.)

WRITING IMPLEMENTS. From various periods. At the back: Wooden palette with empty holes for writing pastes and a slot for writing reeds. Middle Kingdom. Centre: Palette of white marble with coloured pastes, with no space for reeds. New Kingdom. Below: Ceramic inkwells in the shape of cartouches for writing pastes. The cartouche is the oval line that encircles the names of gods and kings. Late period. (Cairo Museum.)

SCRIBE. Already during the Fifth Dynasty the palette was greatly elongated and fitted with a slot to hold the reeds. The water pouch also became long in shape. That humour was not incompatible with the dignity of the scribe's office is shown by this picture. Note the sly expression of this scribe, who has stuck a reserve reed behind his ear. (Tomb of Mehu, 5–6 Dyn., Sakkara.)

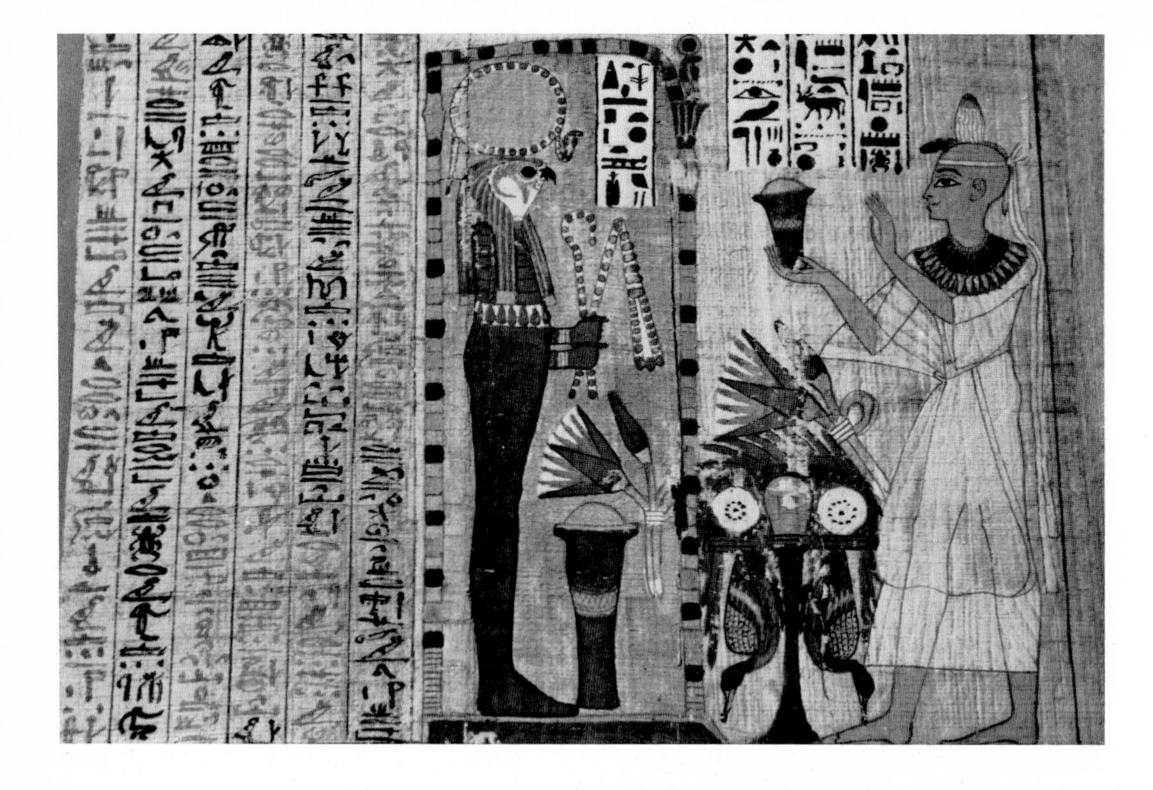

Papyrus. On the left-hand papyrus from the Late period we see on the left side the hieratic script, while the upper part of the coloured drawing shows black hieroglyphs on a white ground. Between the deity Horus-Ra-Harakhte and the celebrant priest stands a table bearing offerings. (Late period, Cairo Museum.)

Registering Wheat. Four land workers are measuring the quantities of heaped up wheat with their wooden containers. Three scribes are registering the amounts under the supervision of a fourth. The importance of the scribes in comparison to the workmen is manifested in their greater size. (Tomb No. 69, Mena, 18 Dyn., Sheikh Abdel Gurna.)

SCRIBES' OFFICE. Practical diligence prevails in this office. We can positively hear the scratching of the reed pens, the rustling of the papyri. The apprentice is leaning forward attentively, a new papyrus scroll in his hand. It is his duty too, as an inscription states, to sprinkle the room with water so that the scribes do not suffer from the heat. (Tomb of Mereruka, Sakkara, 5 Dyn.)

Weighing and Registering. In order to make the contents visible, the scales are shown in cross-section. Weighing had a profound significance, because the gods' judgment on the soul was passed with the aid of a balance. Moreover, the name of the old capital city, Memphis, means "Balance of the World". (Painted relief from Sakkara, 5 Dyn., Cairo Museum.)

Scales. The wooden scales are suspended by four cords of flax. The bronze scale in the centre, on the other hand, has only three chains. (New Kingdom and Late period. Cairo Museum.)

Tax Collecting. A man who owes taxes is dragged before the judge by constables carrying sticks. His left hand is clasping a papyrus scroll: a petition or proof of his innocence. (From Sakkara, 5 Syn., Cairo Museum.)

Cattle Stocktaking. On the roofed platform sits the high official; beside him the scribes with their writing implements. Standing in front of them, at a lower level and separated by the pillars, a bowing countryman. (Painted wooden funerary model from Thebes, Middle Kingdom, Cairo Museum.)

MAN READING. The general term "scribe" is used to cover all pictures of men versed in letters. There are two distinct ways of rendering men writing, either with raised or lowered head. Readers do not hold a reed pen but only the open scroll. They are shown looking up or bending their head over it. In spite of the damage, the thoughtful expression of this reading man is particularly marked. (4–5 Dyn., Cairo Museum)

Painting

Painting with a spatial effect

The otherworldly look

Painting

The designation of the painter as a "writer of the outline" shows how closely painting and writing were linked. As already stated, the written characters consisted largely of outlines of men, animals and plants. For their part, paintings are interspersed with texts. The painter used earth colours for white, yellow, brown and red; metal oxides, i.e. frits, for green and blue; soot for black. The frits have proved least durable; hence green is the colour that has most often faded. The most commonly used binding agent was gum arabic, rarely other vegetable juices. In the New Kingdom paintings and painted woodcarvings were sometimes varnished. As a result of drying out for thousands of years, the layer of varnish has peeled in parts, taking the underlying layer of paint with it and so destroying the painting. For painting in large areas brushes of various sizes made of plant fibre were used; curiously, the hair brush remained unknown to the Egyptians. Instead they used reeds and plant stalks with teased-out tips for outlining and filling in and also as a writing implement.

Proportions

A grid of vertical and horizontal lines, more often visible in reliefs than in wall paintings, did not, as is often supposed, serve the purpose of transposing a small model onto a larger scale, but was used to preserve the proportions of the various parts of the body and limbs and also to maintain the proportions between figures of unequal size. Men are depicted smaller than gods, the subject smaller than his ruler.

It may be permissible here to point to a parallel in Romanesque and Gothic art. The donors of altar panels are depicted on a smaller scale than God the Father, Christ and the Mother of God, archangels larger than the other angels, the worshippers of a Madonna on a rood-screen the size of children.

As the Son of God, the pharaoh was the same size as the gods. Apart from their rounded forms, children are portrayed with the same proportions of head, torso and limbs as adults but on a smaller scale. In surprising contrast to the way it is depicted by other peoples, the pelvis of women is shown as narrower rather than wider in proportion to the shoulders. Broad shoulders and narrow pelvis in women corresponded to an ideal of beauty, not to reality. Fatness was despised, and when it was portrayed at all it was as a curiosity. Exceptions are rare, e.g. the portrait of Rekhmare in his own tomb. Only the Nile at high water is personified as a fat man with a highly developed chest. In general, the artist had to keep to drawing-copies or models. The skin colour was traditional: reddish-brown for men and for women a dull, pale yellow. Yet each epoch brought forth fresh creative energies that broke through tradition.

The Egyptian artist was proud of his work, otherwise the sculptor of the tomb of Pta-hotep (5th Dynasty, Sakkara) would not have portrayed himself and attached his name to the portrait. He is sitting on a reed boat and has evidently earned the drink he has been given. Similar self-portraits placed as a signature under the finished tomb-painting are known from the New Kingdom. The painters sit in negligent postures, as though taking a last critical look at their work. They are distinguished from other people by their uncut hair and long robes that are wound round them.

The Simultaneous Frontal and Profile View

We find in Egypt a peculiar method of portrayal in paintings and reliefs in which the head, arm, lower part of the body and legs are seen in profile, while the upper part of the body and the eye are shown from the frontal view. Nineteenth-century writers attempted to explain this curiously mixed view-point as due to so-called initial errors dating from proto-historical times. Such an explanation is no longer convincing, however, since plenty of examples of a perfect side view occur in the same picture or relief. We too easily forget that most of these representations come from tombs and temples and hence are of a religious character. Today we look upon them as works of art detached from place and purpose, whereas these figures originally represented, for example, participants in a procession or the occupant of a tomb facing his god. Since, according to the ancient Egyptian conception, the heart was the seat of good and evil, and the god sitting in judgment had to see the heart, man had to show him his chest in its full breadth. Uninvolved and secondary figures are shown in unexceptionable profile. In their search for completeness, Egyptian artists tried to preserve everything in its clearest, most permanent form and presented from its most characteristic angle those parts of the body most clearly seen in profile e.g., the head, the arms and the feet, which were drawn that way but the upper part of the body is best seen from the front so as to show the ghingin of the arms to the shoulders. In essence, Egyptian art was not based on what the artist saw at a given moment in time, but rather on what he knew belonged there—forever.

Lighting during work

The nature of the lighting by which craftsmen and artists worked in the depths of the mountain has not yet been established. Certain tombs may be as much as three hundred feet underground. At the same time, the galleries rarely ran straight; more often they were crooked and sloped either upwards or downwards, ending in a chamber that was a great deal loftier than its entrance. The lamps with wicks and the torches that have come down to us from those times would have been impossible to use as working lights because they gave off too much soot and smoke. Not only would they have failed to give sufficient light, but they would also have used up too much oxygen and raised the already considerable temperature in the rock to an unbearable level. No traces of soot have ever been found in undamaged tombs. All layers of smoke and soot date from a later age. Early Christians lived as hermits in the more easily accessible chambers, as the inscriptions and paintings they left behind show. They were followed by Bedouins and peasants. Ever since ancient Egypt became known to Europe through the French expedition (end of the 18th century) an unbroken stream of archeologists, sightseers and unfortunately also tomb robbers have entered with their torches. Electric light has only recently been installed in the majority of the tombs in the Valley of the Kings.

The supposition that daylight was reflected into the tomb chambers by means of a series of bronze mirrors (which incidentally were only the size of hand mirrors) is of limited validity, since the method could have been applied to short distances only. After a certain number of reflections the intensity of the light is so reduced that the amount reaching its final destination would be insufficient to work by. Even if the intensity of the light had been greater, the illuminated area would have been too small to execute works of such gigantic dimensions. And how was the reflected light to enter tombs situated deep down in gorges that faced north? A new theory postulates the use of soot-free lamps fed with alcohol. It is supported upon the knowledge that alcohol was drunk, grapes pressed and beer brewed in ancient Egypt; but fermentation and distillation are based upon different principles. If distillation was really known, why has no trace of any distilling plant ever been found?

Further questions arise out of the unanwered question of lighting. The riddle of how the work was done cannot be dismissed by attributing it to "slaves." One must bear in mind how much intelligent organization was required to hollow out these widely ramified underground chambers, remove the hewn out-rock, get rid of the used air and introduce fresh, to light all the working areas and direct and feed the workers without friction. And one glance at the decorations of these rock-cut tombs is enough to show that they are not the work of prisoners, but the consummate achievements of highly skilled stonemasons, sculptors and painters which could only have been born of a free, creative spirit.

If our age is taking an ever-increasing interest in Egyptian art, this is chiefly due to aesthetic affinities. The painting of flat areas with generally unbroken colour, and the building up of form with no illusion of depth, is in line with modern artistic taste. The naturalness which characterizes the art of early times, and which found sublime expression in the works of the Old Kingdom, is in keeping with modern trends. The need for simplified forms has a magnificent exemplar in the self-enclosed creations of Egyptian art.

On the other hand, the examples must not be arbitrarily detached from their purpose and context. To compare over-enlarged sections of wall-paintings with the still-lifes of contemporary masters is pure fraud. To attempt to deduce a similar spiritual content from the chance similarity of forms is absurd. Every art has its own presuppositions and problems, which grow out of its epoch and environment.

Painting with a spatial effect

The widespread view that in their painting the ancient Egyptians knew only two-dimensional space has developed from initial observation into an axiom. Areas were enclosed by an outline and filled in with flat colour. Perspective in drawing and the illusion of space through the gradation of colours remained unknown, colour and drawing, jointly or separately, never produced anything but a flat-surface effect. Such statements may be generally valid, but they do not hold good in their entirety for the period of the New Kingdom.

One of our reproductions shows a painted relief in which herdsmen with their cows are wading a ford. Above water the bodies are painted an even, strong colour. Below the surface the tone of the legs pales away till it disappears completely. This example from the Old Kingdom—and it is one of several—shows that the effect is deliberate and not due to chance. In the past, attempts have repeatedly been made by younger, unprejudiced experts to demonstrate the presence of perspective effects in Egyptian art. The claim was violently rejected by Egyptologists of the older school. I myself have observed a similar case in the drawing on page 148 from the tomb of Tuthmosis III. Ibis-headed figures are shown standing one behind the other, which in itself does not produce any effect of space. Both the birds' heads with their long beaks and the shoulders slope away downwards, whereas the hands holding the knives are again drawn all on one level, thus creating an illusion of spatial depth. On page 90 of his book *La peinture égyptienne* A. Mekhitarian describes a detail of a wall painting showing the daughter of Menna: "The arms are filled in with dashes that disclose the spontaneity of the work and at the same time reproduce the colour of the suntanned skin and the full forms."

The same tomb contains a painting of a papyrus thicket with a wild cat creeping up on birds' nests. The liveliness of the animal's movements engages all our attention. But if we make the effort to look more closely at the eggs in the nests, we observe a bluish brushline on their lower half. It begins as a point in the upper half of the oval and broadens out towards the bottom, following the curve of the egg. The oval white area shows unmistakable volume.

On page 101 of the above work, the author speaks of a locust: ". . . the yellowish pink on the wings is deeper than on the belly; it is not only true to life, but also creates an impression of space, which is underlined by the curved and parallel lines on the tail." An authority has looked at this art afresh and without preconceptions and has described his observations with compelling clarity.

The Ford. (Tomb of Ti, Sakkara, 5 Dyn.)

Ibis-Headed Figures. (Tomb of Tethmosis III., Valley of the Kings. Thebes, 8 Dyn.)

PASHEDU PRAYING. (Tomb No. 345, Deir el-Medina, 20 Dyn.)

PASHEDU PRAYING. (Detail)

The wall painting from the tomb of Pashedu reproduced on page 149 goes even further than the case described by Mekhitarian. Here too we can see the roundness of the sitter's forearm, but it is the first instance, so far as I know, where a single source of light has been consistently employed. Pashedu is kneeling with upraised hands in a position of prayer, clad only in a loincloth with many folds. Even though this typical posture corresponds to prototypes that had been repeated a thousand times and hence had become stylized, the method of painting is nevertheless remarkably free and unconventional. The brown ground-tone of the body and the white of the garment have been laid in broadly and unconcernedly, without previous drawing. At various points brown and white run over the outlines that were drawn in afterwards, yet no corrections have been made. Only along the two thumbs has white been painted in later to cover up the disturbing patches in the background. In the centre of the upper part of the body a second, dark layer of colour lies like a glaze over the first layer, which shows through. The paint on both sides of the body has been lightly but visibly wiped away before it was quite dry. Parts of the face under the brown and the eye have been similarly treated. On nose, mouth and chin the paint is very thin; at the corner of the mouth it has been strengthened by a brushstroke, producing a palpable arching of the upper lip.

If these effects are to be ascribed to the slapdash approach of an arrogant temperament coupled with consummate technical skill, the perhaps still unconscious but already emergent will to three-dimensionality is unmistakably evident in the projecting shoulder. A clear, broad stroke of considerably lighter colour that has been put on wet follows the contour of the shoulder. The further shoulder, on the other hand, has been rendered relatively paler by a stroke of thin colour. The combination of dots and wavy lines render the mountains that form the background to the scene of prayer. The still fluid paint of the dot immediately over the shoulder has visibly run into the outline of the body. This could have been corrected by covering the run with a fresh layer of paint as in the case of the hands. Instead, the artist has contented himself with laying in the broad band of mixed colour that emphasizes the modelling.

We are bound to ask ourselves why the painter has rendered a light falling on the shoulder. Unfortunately, I have at the moment no colour photograph of the whole wall-painting at my disposal. A small colour reproduction is given on page 15 of A. Lhote's *Les chefs-d'oeuvre de la peinture égyptienne*. Pashedu is praying to the Supreme Judge. To the right above Pashedu two burning torches are to be seen whose reflection, in this particular case, is visible on the shoulders.

Instinctively to grasp and simultaneously bring to realization a new artistic form implies the combined operation of conscious and unconscious factors at the moment of creation. The whole style of the painter's "handwriting" bears witness to great assurance and powerful vitality. This dynamic temperament must have looked with contempt upon petty precision of brushwork. Only such an artist could have so brilliantly seized upon the essentials amidst the interaction of various elements and given them material expression. Such an impulsive manifestation at this period would have been unthinkable without the spiritual and artistic revolution brought about by Akhenaton which preceded it.

"Ancient Egypt was unacquainted with the portrait" is an assertion that for many years had been commonplace. It is still repeated today. As a so-called established fact it is explained by saying that at an early stage the Egyptians gave up individual characterization in favour of a supra-personal mode of representation. This typification is said to be both the strength and weakness of the whole of Egyptian art. To prove this ostensible rule by an exception, reference is made to the Akhenaton era. With its verist tendency it was able to burst asunder petrified tradition and, for the short period of its duration, created truly individual likenesses.

The danger of generalized statements lies in their half-truth. In this case the formula, apart from its

The otherworldly look

partial correctness, offers a comfortable solution to the problems of such a complex style as the ancient Egyptian. The assertion that "the portrait was unknown in ancient Egypt" could easily be refuted by a comprehensive selection of pictorial works, which would not only show clear physical differences but also distinctly marked personalities.

The whole argument proves groundless when we study the tomb statues closely. In their case personal characterization is a necessity required by ritual. If it did not satesfy this precondition the statue would not fulfil its purpose. In the Early Dynastic period the tomb was purely a safe resting-place for the mummy and its funerary objects. With the Third Dynasty it became a sepulchre and at the same time

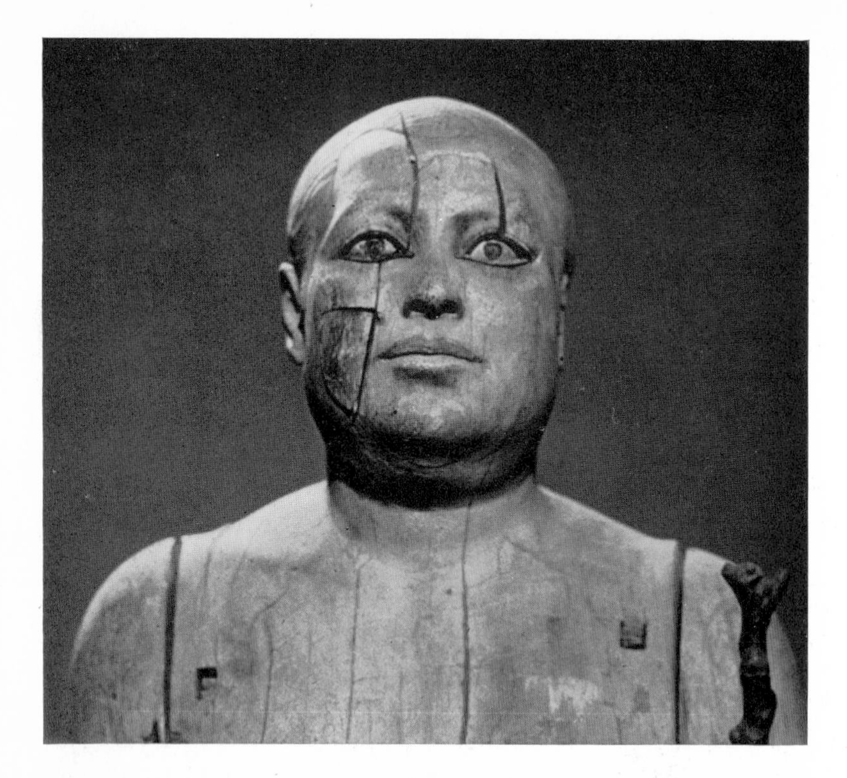

a house for the mortuary statue. The subdivision or separate chamber set aside for it was called the "house of the *Ka*", a term later applied to the whole tomb. The statue, as the visible embodiment of the deceased, was intended to be the dwelling place of his *Ka*. What did this monosyllable mean?

The Egyptians distinguished several mutually independent concepts of the soul, the two chief ones being *Ka* and *Ba*. Our conception of the soul as a single, all-embracing idea standing for the great secret of human life has been laboriously evolved over a period of thousands of years. Hence we find it hard to grasp the ancient Egyptian notion of several distinct souls inhabiting one body. In any case,

KA-APER. Chief steward of the royal estates. Wood with traces of painting; inlaid eyes. Popularly known as *The Sheikh of the Village*. (From Sakkara, 6 Dyn., Cairo Museum)

SCRIBE I. Unknown sceibe, painted limestone. (From Sakkara, 4-5 Dyn., Cairo Museum)

SCRIBE II. Unknown scribe with inlaid eyes. (5 Dyn., Cairo Museum)

Page 151: TUT-ANKH-AMON. Painted wood. (Valley of the Kings, Thebes. 18 Dyn., Cairo Museum)

A Priest in Prayer. Ka-em-Ked. High priest of the Hem-ka. Noteworthy for representing the individual with a full head of hair. In later times, priests were obliged to be rid of body and head hair. Panted limestone with inlaid eyes. (Sakkara, 4-5 Dyn., Cairo Museum)

they cannot be comprehended by means of the conceptual distinctions current in our psychological terminology.

Up to the present, Egyptologists have failed to find an unequivocal definition of the variety of these concepts of the soul or to agree on suitable terms by which to describe them. It is difficult to find a meaning which we can understand for each individual designation. The Egyptians themselves did not seek any unambiguous explanations of them. The distinction between material and ideal, concrete and abstract etc., which we have been taught to make by our analytical mode of thought, could not arise at all as a means of dividing one thing from another in the intellectual heritage of Egypt. To the

Egyptians life, death and resurrection, this world and the next, had much in common, they interpenetrated one another. The explanation offered by Professor J. Spiegel of Göttingen may be the most illuminating for our age. "The *Ka* is the effective power of God, which creates and governs life. It provides the necessary link between God and earth, between cosmic power and earthly phenomena. The statues set up in the tombs are regarded as its visible embodiments."

What has been said regarding the difficulty of clearly defining the *Ka* also applies, up to a point, to the *Akh*. According to the earliest ideas, after a man's death his *Akh* flew up to the night sky, where it blazed out in the firmament as a star on the star-strewn body of the Queen of Heaven. Later the soul-concept *Ba* was depicted as a bird with a human head. It was *Ib*, the heart, that was called upon to answer before the Court of the Dead for a man's deeds on earth. The notion of this Court first emerges at the end of the Fifth Dynasty in *ca.* 2450 B. C. The jurisdiction exercized by the Great God in the Next World was a conception that had existed before that. According to the religious belief then prevalent, the divine order, in conformity with its law, had already conferred his "dignity" upon the chosen individual in his earthly life. This dispensation enabled the man thus singled out to claim the same dignity in the Next World as a right. Desecrators of tombs were threatened with divine or heavenly punishment. As to the lot of the anonymous mass of those who had not attained to "dignity" either through the ruler (as God's earthly son and representative) or through inheritance from their father, we have no information. With changes in the religion the idea of the judgment of the dead underwent a modification. The "man of dignity" became the "man who had justified himself", or failed to justify himself, as the case might be. The right of justification was extended to all believers and no longer confined to a closed circle of "men of dignity."

The *Ka* statue possessed all the essential and characteristic features of its model, otherwise the *Ka* could not accept this figure as its materialization within the tomb. According to its ritual definition it was not a portrait in our sense, not a representation of the individual at a particular stage in his life or in a passing mood. It was an attempt to capture the essence of the individual, to give sculptural expression to his specific, fundamental qualities, and in this sense the *Ka* statue was a complete likeness. Comparisons between mummies that have been preserved and the corresponding statues or reliefs from their tombs show convincing similarities, even from an anatomical point of view, despite the supposed tendency of the Egyptian style to reduce everything to a stereotype.

We now know that the *Ka* statues presented individuals and not schematic types. Moreover, we must bear in mind that the whole furnishing of the tomb was not, like ours, an art means to be looked at, but intended for the interior of the sepulchre that was sunk deep in the rock, walled up and never meant to be seen again by human eyes.

Since these statues symbolized a dead person waiting for the last judgment, the choice of posture, whether standing, sitting, kneeling or squatting, was determined by his piety, rank and profession during his lifetime. In readiness to appear before the All-Highest the figure is always shown full face. Face, chest, pelvis, knees and feet are all pointing in the same direction. If we draw an imaginary vertical, nose, breastbone, navel and crutch all lie on the same line. This frontality has its origin in the position of religious worship and is not, as so often supposed, a heritage of the archaic period, when a certain clumsiness marked the representation of the human figure. The deceased is rendered at an ideal age, and even if he died young he wears an expression of strange maturity. All these sculptures are enveloped by a great quietness, which removes them from the sphere of earthly life. In the era before the Fifth Dynasty they are marked by the self-assurance springing from the "dignity" that is due to them by divine law even in the Next World. Faced by the court of the dead, an expression of doubt and uncertainty over the result of the forthcoming trial is added to that of reverence and surrender.

The otherworldly look is no chance phenomen, it is present in all *Ka* statues of the Old Kingdom. By the Middle Kingdom it is beginning to be forgotten, and it occurs only occasionally in the New Kingdom. Again and again there were periods which consciously harked back to the Old Kingdom, describing it as the "Golden Age" of Egyptian art and reverting to its austere style, without ever equalling it.

In order to see things in the round we need both eyes. Spacial depth is the outcome of the combined images of both eyes. The lateral displacement of the images, that is to say the distance between the axes of the two eyes, produces the new dimension of the object seen; the joint vision of the two eyes from different viewpoints unites to create an idea of space. The clear image of an object comes into being only when the axes of the two eyes converge upon the same point. If perspective is carried to infinity this is shown outwardly by a parallelism of the two eyes. Eyes gazing into the distance, in so far as they are following a straight line, appear to the spectator expressionless—they are gazing into the void. The apparently intense looking becomes staring, it fixes without recognizing. Objectively the otherworldly look could be descibed as one of vague gazing. Without any definite object in view a particular direction of the eyes is held, and at the same time the idea of inward vision is expressed and projected into the infinite. The penetration of indefinite distance takes place with open eyes. Formally, this effect is achieved by a slight vertical, never horizontal, displacement of the pupils in relation to each other. This may be seen by covering up each eye in the illustration in turn.

The rational art of the Greeks and Romans had no call for representation of this kind. The blindness of a seer is rendered by upturned eyeballs devoid of pupils. Gothic art, on the other hand, discovered the Egyptian mode of expression afresh. It sometimes utilizes it in the representation of heavenly figures, singing angels and martyrs, who gaze beatifically up to heaven, ignoring their earthly torments. In Baroque the expression of figures in ecstasy becomes an immobile rolling of both eyes. The last echoes may be found in the meditative, veiled eyes of romantic portraits.

In this brief survey, the attempt has been made to explain why, for religious reasons, the *Ka* statues of the Old Kingdom represented a personal portrait, the likeness of an individual, and not some random ideal type of ancient Egyptian man.

Chronological table

	DYNASTIES	
Archaic Period		
Unification of Upper and Lower Egypt	I–II	*ca.* 3200–2800
Old Kingdom		
First step pyramid	III	*ca.* 2800–2720
The Pyramid Age	IV	*ca.* 2720–2560
The Golden Age of culture and art	V–VI	*ca.* 2560–2270
First Intermediate Period		
Disintegration of the Old Kingdom and serious internal unrest	VII–X	*ca.* 2270–2100
Middle Kingdom		
Unification of the country, lack of balance in art	XI–XIII	*ca.* 2100–1700
Second Intermediate Period		
Invasion and domination by the Hyksos and introduction of the horse and chariot	XIV–XVI	*ca.* 1700–1680
Expulsion of the Hyksos	XVII	*ca.* 1680–1580
New Kingdom		
Empire with tributary states	XVIII	*ca.* 1580–1315
In the beginning an archaizing style, later the culmination of an art with forms of its own		
A striving for classical balance		
Akhenaton's revolution in religion, the verist style degenerating into lyrical decadence		
The gigantic pomp of the Ramessides	XIX–XX	*ca.* 1315–1085
Late Dynastic Period		
Revolt of the tributary states		
A schematic art based on conventional repetition	XXI–XXIV	*ca.* 1085– 715
Ethiopian Occupation	XXV	715–656
Egyptian rulers	XXVI	656–525
First Persian Invasion	XXVII	525–404
Egyptian rulers	XXVIII–XXX	404–341
End of the Dynasties		
Second Persian Occupation		341–333
During the Late Period ancient Egypt inexorably fades away. Repeated attempts to revive the great past end in failure		
Greek and Roman Periods		
The founding of Alexandria	Alexander the Great	332–323
Alexander's successors	The Ptolemies	323–330
Roman Domination		30 B. C.–A. D. 395

Up to the present there is no general agreement as to dates down to the XIXth Dynasty. The attempt to establish them by the position of Sirius at the time of the building of the pyramid of Cheops has not been accepted. Hence we must content ourselves for the present with "*circa*".

Bibliography

Anthes, R., *Lebensregeln und Lebensweisheiten der Alten Ägypter*. Leipzig, 1933

Badawy, A., *A History of Egyptian Architecture*. Cairo 1954

Bonnet, H., *Reallexikon der ägyptischen Religionsgeschichte*. Berlin 1952

Capart, J., *Primitive Art in Egypt*. London 1905

Capart, J., *L'art égyptien*. Brussels 1922/42

Capart, J., *Documents pour servir a l'étude de l'art égyptien*. Paris 1927

Devaud, E., *Les maximes de Ptah-hotep*. Fribourg 1916

Drioton-Vandier, *L'Egypte (les peuples de l'Orient Méditerranéen)*. Paris 1946

Edwards, J. E. S., *The Pyramids of Egypt*. London 1947

Emery, W. B., *Archaic Egypt*. London 1961

Erman, A. *Ägypten und ägyptisches Leben im Altertum*. Rev. ed. by H. Ranke, Tübingen 1923

Frankfort, H., *The Birth of Civilisation in the Near-East*. London 1951

Haman, R., *Ägyptische Kunst*. Berlin 1944

Junker, H., *Die Ägypter (Die Völker des antiken Orients)*. Freiburg i. Br. 1933

Junker, H., *Pyramidenzeit*. Zürich 1941

Kees, H., *Kulturgeschichte des alten Orients: Ägypten*. Munich 1933

Lange-Hirmer, *Ägypten*. Munich 1955

Lhote, A., *Les chefs d'oeuvre de la peinture égyptienne*. Paris 1954

Loret, V., *Notes sur les instruments de musique de l'Egypte ancienne*. Paris 1913

Loret, V., *La flore pharaonique*

Loret, V., *L'ail chez les anciens Egyptiens*

Lucas, A., *Ancient Egyptian Materials*. 2nd ed. London 1934

Maspero, G., *L'Egypte. Histoire générale de l'art*. Paris 1912

Mekhitarian, A., *La peinture égyptienne*. Geneva 1954

Montet, Pierre, *La vie quotidienne en Egypte au temps des Ramses*. Paris 1946

Posener, G., Saumeron et Yoyotte, *Dictionnaire de la civilisation égyptienne*. Paris 1959

Saad, Z. Y., *Excavations at Saqqarah and Helwan*. Cairo 1948

Saad, Z. Y., *Excavations at Helwan*. Cairo 1951

Saad, Z. Y., *Ceiling Stelae in Second Dynasty Tomb*. Cairo 1957

Schäfer, H., *Von ägyptischer Kunst*. Leipzig 1919

Spiegel, J., *Das Werden der altägyptischen Hochkultur*. Heidelberg 1953

Steindorf, G., *Die Blütezeit des Pharaonenreichs*. Bielefeld und Leipzig 1900

Steindorf, G., *Die Kunst der Ägypter*. Leipzig 1928

Vandier, J., *Manuel d'archéologie égyptienne*. Paris 1952

Weigall, A., *A History of the Pharaohs*. London 1925

Wreszinski, W., *Atlas zur altägyptischen Kulturgeschichte*. Leipzig 1915/28

PERIODICALS

Annales du Service des Antiquités de l'Egypte. Cairo I/1900

Bibliotheca aegyptica, Brussels, since 1931

Bulletin de l'Institut français d'Archéologie orientale du Cairo. I/1901

Journal of Egyptian Archeology. London I/1914

Mitteilungen des Deutschen Instituts für ägyptische Altertumskunde in Cairo.

Zeitschrift für ägyptische Sprache und Altertumskunde, Leipzig. I/1863